THE CRAFT OF PETER TAYLOR

THE CRAFT OF PETER TAYLOR

Edited by

C. Ralph Stephens
and
Lynda B. Salamon

The University of Alabama Press

Tuscaloosa and London

Copyright © 1995
The University of Alabama Press
Tuscaloosa, Alabama 35487-0380
All rights reserved
Manufactured in the United States of America

∞

The paper on which this book is printed meets the minimum
requirements of American National Standard for Information
Science-Permanence of Paper for Printed Library Materials,
ANSI Z39.48-1984.

Library of Congress Cataloging-in-Publication Data

The craft of Peter Taylor / edited by C. Ralph Stephens and Lynda B.
    Salamon.
        p.   cm.
    Includes bibliographical references and index.
    ISBN 0-8173-0789-3
        1. Taylor, Peter Hillsman, 1917–   —Criticism and interpretation.
    I. Stephens, C. Ralph (Charles Ralph) II. Salamon, Lynda B., 1942–

PS3539.A9633Z614   1995   94-45774
813'. 54—dc20   CIP

British Library Cataloguing-in-Publication Data available

Contents

Acknowledgments

We are grateful to Essex Community College for its encouragement and support, to our colleagues and families for their advice and patience, to our contributors for their diligence and perseverance, and to our secretary, Terry Walter, for her cheerful assistance with the manuscript. Our greatest debt, however, is to Peter Taylor himself, for producing such a fine body of work and for cooperating so generously in our undertaking.

Abbreviations

Quotations from the major works of Peter Taylor are given in the body of the text with the following abbreviations:

CS   *The Collected Stories of Peter Taylor*

HF   *Happy Families Are All Alike*

LF   *A Long Fourth and Other Stories*

MD   *In the Miro District and Other Stories*

ML   *Miss Leonora When Last Seen and 15 Other Stories*

OF   *The Old Forest and Other Stories*

OSC   *The Oracle at Stoneleigh Court: Stories*

P   *Presences: Seven Dramatic Pieces*

SM   *A Stand in the Mountains*

SUM   *A Summons to Memphis*

WM   *A Woman of Means*

WT   *The Widows of Thornton*

All page references are to the original hardcover editions. Full citations appear in the Works Cited list at the end of this volume.

THE CRAFT OF PETER TAYLOR

Introduction

C. RALPH STEPHENS AND
LYNDA B. SALAMON

ALTHOUGH PETER TAYLOR has been writing for more than fifty years, public recognition has been slow in coming. Critical acclaim, however, is another matter. In 1986, Taylor was awarded a Pulitzer Prize for his novel *A Summons to Memphis*. He also has won PEN/Faulkner and PEN/Malamud awards; an O. Henry Memorial Award; a Ritz Hemingway Prize for fiction; and Guggenheim, Fulbright, National Institute of Arts and Letters, National Endowment for the Arts, and Ford and Rockefeller fellowships and grants. It was only following the publication of *A Summons to Memphis,* as Hubert H. McAlexander points out in the very useful bibliographic essay that serves as an introduction to his 1993 *Critical Essays on Peter Taylor,* that Taylor's work began to appear regularly in anthologies and claimed the attention of a wide audience of readers. Surely such attention was long overdue. Novelist Madison Smartt Bell has described Taylor as "arguably the best American short story writer of all time," and Anne Tyler has declared: "A century from now, when our descendants look back and marvel at our ignorance, they might very well mention the relative lack of homage we paid to Peter Taylor. He is, after all, the undisputed master of the short story form."

This volume is an attempt to remedy "our ignorance" concerning Peter Taylor. It grew out of a Baltimore symposium on Taylor, sponsored by Essex Community College in April 1991, which drew together scholars from across the country and from abroad who shared a deep admiration for this distinguished man of letters. Some of the pieces collected in this volume (those by Griffith, Hardwick, Scott, Metress, Richmond, Nelson, McAlexander, Lynn, Wilson, and Bell) have been developed from papers read at the symposium; others (those by Lindsay, Robinson, Kuehl, Beattie, Brinkmeyer, and Brooks) have been written especially for this book. All are original. The arrangement of chapters within the volume is as follows: considerations of Taylor's work in general or of themes common to several of his works appear first and are followed by considerations of specific works (in order of their publication dates); reminiscences by acquaintances come next; and an interview with Peter Taylor conducted by Christopher Metress in August 1993 concludes the volume. We hope that this first book-length collection of original essays, which direct attention to a variety of themes and techniques in a broad cross section of Taylor's work, will encourage critical discussion and provide a foundation for further study.

In the opening essay, Albert J. Griffith explores Taylor's "personal poetics." Although Taylor early eschewed writing criticism, he has in fact become over the years a teacher and theorist with a coherent aesthetic that can be retrieved from several sources: from his stories dealing with art or artists, from a few published reminiscences, from interviews, and from his occasional essays. According to Griffith, Taylor's poetics grow from the idea that "nearly everything about art is a mystery" and the notion that what is fundamentally unknowable is essential to art. Griffith also considers Taylor's role as a Southern writer, one who shows how different Southerners are and at the same time asserts the universality of their experience. As a Southerner, Taylor recognized that a momentous change was occurring as modernization brought about the decline of the family and the farm. Although he illustrated the effects of this change in the South, it was in fact a more general change, and in tracing it, Taylor has succeeded in relating the particular to the universal.

In an essay derived from her keynote address at the Baltimore symposium, Taylor's longtime friend Elizabeth Hardwick also examines the centrality of place in Peter Taylor's stories, so often concerned with "a location within a location . . . that is, with particular streets and [a particular] residence on them." "No one," she writes, "has used this location within the location as tellingly as Peter Taylor." She discusses "The Old Forest," *A Summons to Memphis,* and several short stories, illustrating Taylor's function as "a sort of casual historian of the middle-sized cities of the Upper South."

The relationship between Taylor and the Agrarians is the focus of Ward Scott's essay, which illustrates how the "rich and complicated" issues of *I'll Take My Stand* are clearly reflected in "What You Hear from 'Em?" Aunt Munsie, the story's protagonist, embodies the decline of the agrarian lifestyle and laments the lack of "quality" people to be found in an increasingly industrialized society. Her banishment from the streets of Thornton, where she and her slop wagon have for years been familiar sights, signals the ascendancy of a new society in which motor vehicles are afforded more concern than human beings.

Creighton Lindsay's reading of Peter Taylor's work in the context of the tradition of the American pastoral draws on recent work by Lawrence Buell. Taylor's mastery is evident, Lindsay argues, in the variations he is able to work on the pastoral theme, particularly in his use of "inverted pastoral insets" in which "a bucolic opportunity" is presented only to be denied. Narrators such as Phillip Carver in *A Summons to Memphis,* for example, may choose to alienate themselves from pastoral landscapes, in this case "escaping" to New York City. Lindsay shows how Taylor expands the conventional notion of the pastoral by substituting for the traditional image of the garden an image of wild nature, as he does, for example, in "The Old Forest." Lindsay's identification of instances in which Taylor "teases the mode" of the pastoral provides readers and critics with a fresh perspective from which to view the works.

According to Christopher Metress, a knowledge of "absence" is central to understanding Taylor's fiction; what is missing from certain images "reveals everything and fills that which is present with greater significance." Meaning must then be "negotiated" from the awareness of these absences. In support of his thesis, Metress draws on "Two Pilgrims," in which the narrator must learn both to see what is not there and to hear what is left untold; *Presences,* Taylor's collection of plays in which the "presences" are really absences because they are ghosts; and a group of stories, including "What You Hear from 'Em?" "Miss Leonora When Last Seen," and the more recently published "Cousin Aubrey," in which Taylor employs a "figure of absence," someone whose absence or disappearance "generates not only anxiety but also the narrative itself." Metress concludes with a consideration of absence in *The Oracle at Stoneleigh Court.*

Informed by the theories of Freud and Lacan, Linda Richmond focuses on the theme of betrayal in "Dean of Men" and *A Summons to Memphis.* She analyzes the psychological devastation wrought when young boys (the narrator in the short story and the protagonist in the novel) witness the betrayal of their fathers by a trusted friend and business associate. The paternal figure, she argues, has the power to determine his children's identities and the societal roles they will assume, and she shows how each work illustrates this.

David Robinson's analysis of "The Other Times" begins the section of the volume devoted to considerations of specific works by Peter Taylor. Beginning by acknowledging the similarities between Aunt Martha's Tavern in "The Other Times" and The Cellar in "The Old Forest," Robinson suggests that the two stories share a similar theme as well; in the quest for maturity, each narrator moves in a dual world in which a familiar milieu marked by artificial social distinctions contrasts with a marginal world that more closely parallels harsh "reality." It is in the latter of these worlds that the narrators' maturity may be tested. In "The Other Times," the failure to mature is reflected at the end of the story by the narrator's insensitivity to the heroism of the coach, Lou Ramsey, who selflessly allows himself to be caught in the police raid so that the young people can escape. The narrator's insensitivity and lack of self-knowledge link him with many of Taylor's other narrators whose retrospectives show that they, too, have never fully comprehended the past events in which their characters were forged.

Although best known for his short fiction, Peter Taylor has worked in other genres as well, notably verse and drama. Ronald Nelson examines four of Taylor's "stoems" from *In the Miro District,* finding in "Her Need," "Three

Heroines," "The Hand of Emmagene," and "The Instruction of a Mistress" characters who struggle to free themselves from restricting forces. In their refusal to be passive victims, these characters are elevated to tragic status, even though their liberating efforts often fail.

In "Emmagene's Killing Cousins," Linda Kandel Keuhl offers another close reading of one of Taylor's stoems, arguing that in "The Hand of Emmagene," the genteel first-person point of view functions both to modulate the melodrama and to enhance the irony of the work. Telling the tale of his country cousin's grotesque suicide, the narrator unconsciously reveals his own betrayal of her and demonstrates his culpability in her death. He shares his short-sightedness and self-deception with a great many other Taylor narrators, illustrating once again that "the most 'civilized' human beings in Taylor's works are often the most dangerous." (Madison Smartt Bell's reminiscence, which appears later in the volume, provides an interesting description of audience reaction to Taylor's reading of "The Hand of Emmagene.")

Hubert McAlexander contends that Taylor's drama *A Stand in the Mountains* has yet to receive the critical attention it deserves. Analyzing the themes in the play, McAlexander states that "nowhere are the central obsessions of the Taylor canon—history, gender, and the family—brought together in a more disturbing way." Here, Taylor creates a complex play in which he interweaves the themes of modernization (represented by the image of a highway threatening to encroach on a mountain community), gender (represented in the tensions that threaten to undermine the patriarchal order), and family (represented in the violence that ultimately shatters the lives of the play's central characters). McAlexander asserts that this play should be recognized as central to the Taylor canon because its publication marks a shift in Taylor's focus from female to male characters in his constant probing of patriarchal society, the roles it imposes, and the consequences of its decline.

Next, novelist Ann Beattie analyzes brilliantly the complexity Taylor creates in "The Old Forest," observing that the author is "a real master of possibilities, a writer so sure of timing and trajectory, so able to sense the inevitable form of his . . . story, that he can't resist setting an obstacle course for himself." It is through manipulation of this very complexity, Beattie contends, that Peter Taylor is able so skillfully and so completely to "entrap" the reader in his fiction.

Recalling that Taylor has said that all writing represents an attempt to understand life, Robert H. Brinkmeyer, Jr., reads the "endless remembering" of Taylor's retrospective narrators as attempts to "destabilize the authoritarian self." In his reading of *A Summons to Memphis*, Brinkmeyer argues persuasively that Phillip Carver's one-dimensional view of his father as tyrannical is tested and reshaped through the linked processes of remembering and writing as Phillip eventually reaches for understanding of the older man. Although

Phillip appears to be moving from authoritarian author to cognitive author, in fact the conclusion of the story illustrates that he falls short.

While we have grouped the foregoing articles into categories of general and specific considerations, they might as easily have been grouped thematically, for they cluster about several main concerns in Taylor criticism (many of which are identified in Albert Griffith's introductory essay). Several of the articles probe the complexity of Taylor's work, a complexity that Griffith identifies and Taylor affirms as growing out of his conviction that in life as in art there are no easy answers. This realization leads Taylor to create stories with multiple levels, such as "The Old Forest," the subject of Ann Beattie's analysis, or stories in which meaning must be inferred, as Christopher Metress argues. A contributing factor to the complexity of Taylor's stories is his adoption of a complicated narrative point of view. "Unreliable" is far too simple a term for these usually complacent middle-aged men whose retrospectives often reveal their inabilities (or refusals) to achieve self-knowledge. David Robinson, Linda Kandel Kuehl, and Robert Brinkmeyer illustrate ways in which Taylor lays bare the shortcomings of such narrators. In addition, various articles collected here relate to Taylor's role as "historian of the middle-sized cities of the Upper South" (in Elizabeth Hardwick's phrase). Ward Scott and Hubert McAlexander address Taylor's concern with the modernization of the rural South and its effect on once-strong family structures, and Linda Richmond offers a different perspective on the deterioration of the family in her psychological reading. These connections (and others that readers may discover for themselves) both enhance previous scholarship and offer grounds for new research.

However, although the critical articles collected here suggest several avenues for further examination of Peter Taylor and his works, there are significant "absences" in the collection that point (in the best Taylor fashion) to other areas of exploration. There has, for example, been scant previous attention to works like the stoems and the plays—both *Presences* and, especially, *Tennessee Day in St. Louis* are fertile areas, and a new focus on *A Stand in the Mountains* would be especially relevant now that Taylor is reworking it as a novel. No feminist reading of Taylor is included, and surely such a perspective is warranted and would be provocative, particularly in light of Taylor's early use of the female point of view. Nor does this volume contain much work illustrating Taylor's relationship to other writers; if, as Albert Griffith argues in his essay, Taylor has created a "coherent aesthetic" in his decades of teaching and writing, certainly consideration of his influence on other writers would be useful. Finally, though Taylor has expressed his displeasure at being labeled a "Southern writer," detailed consideration of his place among and connection to other Southern figures is overdue. The critical essays in this volume are by no means definitive, then, but rather are intended to open new areas of inquiry and provoke further discussion.

Following the critical articles is a series of reminiscences by friends, students, and a teacher of Peter Taylor. Cleanth Brooks remembers meeting Taylor as a very young writer who came to Louisiana State University for graduate work in 1940, and he recalls incidents in their long acquaintance. David Lynn, consulting editor for *The Kenyon Review,* describes Taylor's relationship with Kenyon College, where Taylor was an undergraduate and later a member of the faculty and advisory editor of the *Review.* Robert Wilson, of *USA Today,* discusses his friendship with Peter Taylor and expresses his personal reaction to several of Taylor's stories. Novelist Madison Smartt Bell recounts the contrasting reactions of two different audiences on hearing Taylor's reading of "The Hand of Emmagene."

Throughout the reminiscences, as throughout this collection as a whole, flows a deep respect for Peter Taylor, his works, and his career. We believe it appropriate that Peter Taylor himself be given the last word in the volume, and so we close with a recent interview in which Taylor discusses, among other things, his then most recently published collection, *The Oracle at Stoneleigh Court,* as well as two works in progress—a novel based on his story "Cousin Aubrey" and another based on the play *A Stand in the Mountains.* Taylor comments on his use in *The Oracle at Stoneleigh Court* of a narrator who resists making sense of the past, reflecting his own awareness "that it is so very difficult to understand things." His focus in this work on "the mysterious" resonates with the themes Albert Griffith identified in this volume's initial chapter, "The Mystery of Art." The resonance is enhanced by Taylor's remarks on his works in progress, both of which use narrators who must break with convention in order to pursue their art. At the end of the interview, Taylor is asked whether he thinks he will someday understand all of the stories he has told, and he answers, "One or two perhaps, but all? I hope not." It is this sense of continual wonder, this compulsion to probe for understanding even while he realizes that art, like life itself, is essentially a mystery, that has at long last earned Peter Taylor a portion of the recognition he so richly deserves.

General Critical Essays

The Mystery of Art

Peter Taylor's Poetics

ALBERT J. GRIFFITH

For someone whose entire adulthood has been spent not only as a literary practitioner but also as a teacher of writing, Peter Taylor has written comparatively little about his art and his personal aesthetics. Perhaps his reticence in this area should not be surprising. After writing a review of Allen Tate's *The Fathers* while still a student at Kenyon in 1939, Taylor vowed he "would never write another line of criticism" (qtd. in Goodwin, *Conversations* 19). His reasons are clear enough: "Writing criticism takes as much time as writing fiction and is a much less serious business! Teaching takes as much of my life as I want to give to generalization. And I like teaching so much more than I like criticism. . . . And then, too, I have a horror of defining, of limiting. Everything seems to me to be such a cliché as soon as I say it. And the other thing is, as soon as I make a point, I am sure I can disprove it, am sure that the opposite is also true!" (qtd. in Thompson 153–54). If Taylor distrusts his own criticism, he is hardly more sanguine concerning the criticism of others. "I've never learned anything from critics, that is, from people writing about my work," he has said. "I think one of the difficulties is that literary criticism is in the same medium as its subject. . . . [T]he critic writes with words, which are used in writing stories or poems, and there's really a certain competition. Also, the best criticism is poetry and literature itself. . . . so it's not a distinctly separate thing" (qtd. in Ross 490). Much modern criticism, though, he says elsewhere, is not only not literature, but is "antiart, antiliterature"; it "leaves [him] cold," doesn't "make sense," is not even "benign" (qtd. in Robison 138).

This lack of enthusiasm for criticism has not kept Taylor totally silent, however, on issues of critical theory. His students have reported how much he could convey in a classroom about the nature of art—not through lecturing as a self-infatuate authority, but simply through story reading and through kind and generous commentary. Stephen Goodwin remembers: "And though his comments nearly always had to do with the story's surface, and he never spoke of 'form' or 'theme,' it was always clear that important activity was going on below the surface. He seemed to think of a story as a net to be cast wide and dragged deep until it filled with startling, shining life" ("Like Nothing" 56). John Casey adds: "Here at last was someone talking technically about stories with genial authority and at the same time acknowledging, rendering the mysterious power of art" (74).

It would no doubt take the combined memories of all those generations of students who through the years sat at the master's feet to bring together all the wit and wisdom Taylor may have dispensed about the great mystery of literary art. Still, it may be useful to peruse those ideas of Taylor's about literature, creativity, and aesthetics that have made it into print and to try to see just what kind of personal poetics they seem to represent. These ideas must be retrieved in fragments, though, from a disparate batch of sources: from the handful of his own stories in which he deals directly or obliquely with writers or other artists, from a few published reminiscences of his students and friends, from his many interviews, and from the rather obscure miscellany of his essays and occasional pieces.

Although few characters in his works speak as writers or artists, he uses at least four to articulate distinctly different positions about the relationship of art and experience. The youthful college boy in the short story "1939" thinks exotic adventure the sine qua non of art: "We wanted to be writers, and we knew well enough that before we could write we had to have 'mature and adult experience' " (*HF* 219-20). The middle-aged artist manqué Frank Lacy in the dramatic piece *The Early Guest* avers, contrariwise, that a writer must stay among the things he knows and loves best—or else never be "able to take [his] own experience quite seriously" (37). And the mature and successful novelist Virgil Minor in the one-act play "Missing Person" argues that environment and experience are less important to the writer than simple peace of mind: "When our work goes well, when we're inspired, we get the notion that our surroundings and the other conditions of our life have something to do with it. . . . But there comes a time when your pattern of work is clearly what counts and you know that what you need from life is not stimulation but rather the tranquillity and the quiet satisfaction of life that will allow you to work" (*P* 70-71).

Perhaps, however, it is the narrator in the story-poem "Knowing" who makes the most astute comment on this issue:

I wake from my dream
And remember everything and wonder
How can anyone imagine knowledge means anything
Or that it is more or less
Than instinct we possess.
Like the others all around us
We know nothing and everything from the beginning.
The day we are born
It's all there.

We are finches and fieldmice
We are beavers and barn owls
We are the cat curled, purring at my feet,
Knowing, knowing, knowing.

    (100)

"It's all there," Peter Taylor has this character propose for our consideration—all we need to know to become writers and artists or anything else—all there, like instinct, from our very beginnings.

Yet, as his comments elsewhere will demonstrate, for Peter Taylor this knowledge is not ordinary knowledge of everyday things but the knowledge of what is fundamentally unknowable. It is the consciousness of mystery: the mystery of life and the mystery of art. The dominant theme that will run through his diverse discourses on writing is that "nearly everything about art is a mystery" and that the practice of art cannot be reduced to professional formulas.

Still, even in this realm of mystery, a skilled practitioner of Taylor's experience and sensitivity cannot help penetrating some of art's mystery with forceful insights about discipline, inspiration, and creative compulsion; about content, form, and style; about plot, character, and theme; and about region, tradition, and history. Taken as a whole, Taylor's theoretical and critical observations can create a new perspective on the choices he has made in his own writing—in a body of work that spans fifty years, stretches the boundaries of several genres, and merits comparison with the work of some of the foremost writers of this century.

The question of the methodology of the writer is perhaps the topic Taylor feels most comfortable with because he can avoid pontificating from on high and can draw on his own down-to-earth experience:

> I don't use any outline or notes. I just begin with the first sentence, first paragraph, and by the time I have a page or two—and that may take some while, at any rate—the margins are just crawling with things I've jotted down. What happens later in the story—the incidents, characterization, lines of dialogue—often comes from those messages I've written myself at the beginning. I don't mean to say that the whole story reveals itself in that first burst of energy, in those first pages. I wish it did. I usually have to wait for a second inspiration before I know how a story will end. The story may have taken a direction I hadn't foreseen, or I may have gotten interested in a different aspect of it, or the original may simply go bad—all sorts of things can divert that first impulse. (qtd. in Goodwin, "An Interview" 9)

Revising follows, he says, and he sometimes throws away as much as ten times what he actually keeps (Kernan 6).

Although his daily regimen for writing demonstrates his earnestness about his task, Taylor has many times made clear that he dislikes being called a "professional," a term he equates with "careerist," which in turn he seems to equate with "commercial hack":

> I don't believe in working, you know. I do my writing the way ladies do their knitting. I just have it around handy, when there's an odd moment. . . .
>
> The main thing is that I work differently at different points in a story. At certain points in the story—toward the end, for example—I work around the clock. But I don't believe that people ought to produce stories or poems the way they produce automobiles. I don't really believe in professionalism. It's one of the subjects about which I'm rabid. Some people think they have to turn out a story or a book a year to be a writer in the professional sense. They're careerists, really. I write whenever I get an idea. . . . I don't think I'm a professional or an amateur; I think I'm an inspired idiot. I just write. As they say in the country, "I do like I know." (qtd. in Daniel 41–42)

But where do the ideas come from that inspire him to take pen in hand? "You don't have to worry about the content—your ideas will come out, just as they do in your dreams," he has said (qtd. in Brickhouse 52). The initial impetus may be something he has experienced or a story or an anecdote he has heard—something close to his own life. "A Spinster's Tale," he says, came "right out of my mother's mouth" (qtd. in Goodwin, "An Interview" 10); much of "Their Losses" and "Two Pilgrims" came verbatim from old stories handed down to him (11); "The Hand of Emmagene" evolved from a bizarre anecdote about the unexplained self-mutilation of a young girl (Brickhouse 52; Thompson 144); "In the Miro District" merged stories about both of his grandfathers (Davis 23–24). "If something sticks in my mind for months and years, I know it must be important to me," he acknowledges (qtd. in Brickhouse 52; see also Thompson 143). However, ever since his father once complained that people could identify his characters, he says he tries "to mix the people and the places up so that they cannot be identified" (qtd. in Davis 24). He also says he eschews research on historical or geographical detail, preferring the memory he has of something to its literal reality (Thompson 151).

People and places are indeed often his beginning point. "[I]t seems to me that what I'm trying to do in my stories is to look at the characters from several points of view, to make sure that I'm at a distance so that I can discover what this character's like and to look at it," he says (qtd. in Smith 63). "A writer uses his models just as a painter might use a model who's come to pose for him," he says elsewhere, but a writer is really "not interested in an exact likeness," and so he "distorts, composes, invents what he needs for the sake of the picture" and thus transforms his original models "into something quite different" (qtd. in Goodwin, "An Interview" 11). The "real poetry" in character creation, he finds, "emerges in the coincidence between the context and the character, as in Chekhov's stories" (qtd. in Smith 64), and he argues that "character and emotional content should always be the strong elements" in every story (qtd. in Thompson 151).

In his youth, Taylor says, he tended to think too much emphasis on plot was "a vulgarity," though he has since become "rather fond of building up a plot" (qtd. in Brickhouse 52). He admits that he has "systematically" worked out some allegorical stories—like "Venus, Cupid, Folly and Time" and "Miss Leonora When Last Seen"—"just the way you'd work out a theorem" (qtd. in Goodwin, "An Interview" 12; see also Thompson 157–58). Nevertheless, he has never allowed a story he once wrote on demand for *The New Yorker* to be reprinted; he has, he insists, "a horror of formulas" (qtd. in DuPree 58).

Clearly Taylor thinks theme rather than plot should determine the direction a story takes. Although he may have one ending in mind when he begins, he may discover others as he works: "I always have some idea, but I think it's important to keep your story free when you are writing it, rather than working mechanically towards a fixed ending. I often reverse my understanding in the course of writing a story. Perhaps my real feelings come out as I write" (qtd. in Thompson 142). He advises strongly that a writer should never try to "make a story go." "I very seldom end by writing the story I set out to write, but I think it's because I'm interested in discovering what I think about something," he says. He cites how his stories about blacks and women (which are now noted for their great empathy and understanding) were not written from any "flaming liberal" ideology but emerged from the discovery he only made while he was writing—the discovery of "who was getting the short end of the stick" in the particular cultural context he was exploring (qtd. in Robison 137; see also Thompson 141–42 and Broadway 78, 87). With regard to the few times he has had "a body of ideas" and "put them in a story consciously," he says that the forced intrusion has "killed" the stories (qtd. in Thompson 151). In looking back on his early work, in fact, Taylor says his principal regret is that he "lacked knowledge" of both what he wanted to say and how to say it, that he "never pressed hard enough" to know what a story meant, and that he consequently "wasted many years of effort writing things that were not the kinds of stories [he] should have been writing" (qtd. in Thompson 171–72).

And what kinds of stories does Taylor think he should have been writing all along? Perhaps the answer to that question is best expressed in Taylor's 1972 University of the South Founder's Day address, titled *Literature, Sewanee, and the World*. In this beautiful and eloquent disquisition (which, except for an abridged local newspaper version, is available only in a tiny 100-copy limited edition chapbook published by the University of the South), Taylor uses an encomium on the *Sewanee Review* literary journal as a vehicle for expressing his view of the role of modern world literature in general and of contemporary Southern literature in particular:

The role of Southern literature has, in some measure, been to discover how we are different and perhaps to assert our difference. But equally and simultaneously it has been to assert the universality of our experience. And that is the nature and concern of all literature. The theme of any profound work of art is to be found in the relation of the particular to the general, the particular to the universal. . . . [I]f the particular and its accurate rendition in his work is the first special concern of the artist, then the modern world and its war on particularity and individuality and eccentricity, its insistence upon uniformity . . . [and] the subjugation . . . of all thought to political thought, that world is the enemy of art; and the artist, the poet, the fiction writer must make his own kind of war upon that world if he and his art are to survive. ([2–3])

To back up these observations, Taylor turns to his own experience as a writer from the state of Tennessee. "I consider the fiction I have written merely a by-product of my efforts to understand who and what I am," he insists. "My feelings are both that this region of the upper South is very much a part of me and that I am very much a part of it" ([3]). Through his knowledge of the particularity of his home region—"I can spend hours gassing to my children about the difference between Memphis and Nashville, Nashville and Knoxville, Knoxville and Chattanooga"—he finds his own knowledge of the universal. Such deep immersion in a rich cultural background, he suggests, gives him and other Southern writers a defense against "a kind of new puritanism, with all the self-righteousness and all the tyranny over men's minds which that implies." And that peculiarly Southern defense, he says, is "a sense of humor, a sense of character, a sense of history, a sense of the mystery of life" ([7]).

In various interviews Taylor has also shown how important place is to him as a writer. In 1987, for instance, he told *Memphis* magazine: "I think the business of a novelist is to make the differences between places seem significant. So when you get to writing about 'place' in fiction, you want to make that place seem as distinctive as you can. You use the paraphernalia of life—the local color—to make the story seem real. As I was writing *A Summons to Memphis,* I had a lot of fun seeing how much I could get into the contrasts between two different places, and then making the story be one that made use of those contrasts" (qtd. in Sides 133).

Of course, Taylor is almost as interested in the past of places he writes about as he is in the present. He makes it clear that he does not quite buy the "delightful Victorian concept that things are getting better and better" or its corollary that "the contemporary equals the excellent" (qtd. in Coffey 29). He values history, he says, because history gives "a sense of how the past affects the present." For Taylor, when fiction draws on history, it says that "life is not just chaos" but "means something." The fiction writer tries to see "sense in events" and "how the way things go influences character." "That's the reason one can go on writing," he adds, "—to make these discoveries about the past and the present" (qtd. in Brickhouse 52).

Despite his eloquent defense of Southern literature in his Sewanee address and despite his frequent disquisitions about the importance of place to literature, Taylor resents critical oversimplifications of his position: "I don't think of myself as a regional writer and I don't really like it when people say, 'He writes about the urban South.' I'm writing about people under certain circumstances, but I'm always concerned with the individual experience and the unique experience of that story. Goodness knows I don't have any political vision for the South, in retrospect or in the future, but I have strong feelings about it. And I think that's the main thing that you have to write about, not only what you have ideas about but what you feel about most keenly" (qtd. in Ross 489).

Taylor attributes the significance of Southern writing to its awareness of a dramatic change that was affecting the whole world—the same kind of circumstances Chekhov wrote about—where "people . . . are ineffectual" and their "whole society doesn't work":

> Faulkner and the other writers, the Agrarians generally, defined this [change]. They could see it. They didn't speak for the world—in fact the Nashville Agrarians were saying it was a Southern phenomenon—but the fact is, it was going on all over the world. . . . There was resistance to this change, to the modernization of society which foresaw the end of the family when the family was no longer a viable economic unit, when the farm was no longer the principal economy. The rest of the world had families too, but the South saw the family changing and focused on that. . . . That's *why* the rest of the world found it fascinating, even though the world might not have known why it was fascinated. I don't think the critics took the line that "this is what is happening to the world," but it was so. And I think that's the way writers find their best subjects. I don't mean they set about to do it, but when a writer becomes as good as Faulkner, it's because there has been a wonderful amazing coincidence between his themes and the circumstances of his day. (qtd. in Thompson 166–67)

In Taylor's own work, this "amazing coincidence" is found in his treatment of the family: "The reason the South interests me primarily is that I think of it in terms of the family" (qtd. in Robison 143). Because of the pace of change in this institution, however, Taylor's family theme has had to shift focus over the years: "It's [now] a different world from the world I began writing about where families did exist as little groups, and if they went out of the South, they took the South with them. It's true to a far lesser degree now. The concern now is for what sort of adjustments we are making to this, how we shall live without it" (qtd. in Thompson 168; see also Broadway 95–96).

One other key link to the South that Taylor often discusses involves the

South's oral storytelling tradition. "I grew up in a family of storytellers," he says. "I listened all the time. Lots of times it didn't make any sense—but a tale or a joke will stick with me for years" (qtd. in M. Jones). Elsewhere he elaborates on this storytelling milieu he grew up in: "My theory is that you listen to people talk when you're a child—a Southerner does especially—and they tell stories and stories and stories, and you feel those stories must mean something. So, really, writing becomes an effort to find out what *all* the stories you hear or think of mean. The story you write is interpretation. People tell the same stories over and over, with the same vocabulary and the same important points, and I don't think it ever crosses their minds what they mean. But they do mean something, and I'm sure that is what influenced me. Then, too, you just inherit a storytelling urge" (qtd. in Ross 489; see also "Short Stories" 13). So strong is that urge that Taylor admits to a period "when I tried to see if I could make every speech in the dialogue in a story one that I had heard somewhere" (qtd. in Goodwin, "An Interview" 10). He also argues, "One of the first rules of dialogue is that a line has to do more than just give information; it has to suggest the sound of a voice, has to be a characteristic speech" (20–21).

Perhaps it is his relish for the oral tale and the sound of the human voice that has led Taylor to choose the short story as his primary literary genre and to defend that form so firmly in his public commentaries on writing. Because Taylor has also tried his hand at novels, drama, and verse, many of his discussions of the short story contrast it with these other literary forms. "I think writing short fiction is much nearer to poetry, than for instance, a novel," he has said. "It must be very tightly written. Everything has to be saying two or three things at once. A lyric poem must be doing more work than a novel. You can't sustain the intensity [of language] in a novel that you do in a short story" (qtd. in Dean 33).

His study of poetry under John Crowe Ransom at Kenyon College taught him the virtue of compression. "When you write poetry you have to make a word count for more, a line count for more," he says. "In a certain way a short story is somewhere between a novel and a poem. Chekhov's stories are really poems. The best stories can be talked about as poems in the same way. You see the structure, you see it all at once, as you can't in the novel" (qtd. in Daniel 44). His related belief that "everything in a work of art must be functional, must contribute, must be working" has led him to be "bored by novels that do less with a chapter than a short story does with a sentence": "More than half of the contemporary novels that I read could have been done more effectively as stories. . . . I believe that a long narrative, a novel, has to do as much more than a short story as an epic poem does than a lyric poem" (qtd. in Goodwin, "An Interview" 16). Taylor is also intrigued by the "real affinity" between drama and fiction and by the fact so many great short story writers (including Chekhov and Pirandello) were also playwrights rather than novelists (Broadway 99–100; see also Thompson 162–63).

Taylor's reflections on these similarities and differences among genres cast light on his experimentation with genre boundaries in his own work. Although he has often cited his preference (as both reader and writer) for short stories over novels and has expressed his resentment of the pressure on short story writers to become novelists, he has not only published the novels *A Woman of Means* and *A Summons to Memphis* but has also started several others (including one he discarded as a novel but later synopsized in the short play *The Early Guest*). In a 1987 interview Taylor said that "it fascinates me that my stories get longer and longer when I'm always trying to make them shorter and shorter," but he also acknowledged that he has decided simply to "go ahead" with this tendency toward greater length, largely because of his increasing interest in plot (Thompson 160, 163–64). He has also accepted Robert Towers's designation of some of his more recent works as "miniature novels": "I thought of them that way to some extent, of suggesting a whole world. . . . I got some ideas of doing that from some Thomas Mann stories and Tolstoy's short novels" (qtd. in Broadway 77–78).

Thus Taylor appears convinced, on the one hand, that a short story's special distinction among fictional genres lies in its compression and in its making every word and every line count for more. But he has also acknowledged, on the other hand, that his own work has moved toward longer and longer fictional forms. This paradox is no doubt what has led him to his most interesting experimental technique—the technique of writing his narratives as if each line were a line of verse, with all the attention to sound, sensual imagery, and symbolic resonance that poetry demands. Some of the works he has written this way—including four stories in *In the Miro District*—he has published in verse format; his friend Robert Lowell called them "story poems," but he himself calls them "broken-line prose" (Thompson 160; Daniel 44) or "stoems" (Wilson [iv]). More intriguing than the publication of a few works in this verse format, however, is his revelation that most of his recent works—including some of the long stories that have been called "miniature novels" and the authentic novel *A Summons to Memphis*—were written (at least in part) as lines of verse and then reformatted for publication to appear on the page as ordinary prose.

Taylor has described his playing with the broken-line prose form in several interviews, including those by Ruth Dean (33), Robert Daniel (44–45), Wendy Smith (61), and Barbara Thompson (160–61, 165–66). The various accounts agree on most particulars, but Thompson records the fullest explanation of his new process: "I began by wanting to get interest in every line, every sentence. I felt if a line is broken, if where the line ends means something, you get another emphasis. When a sentence just ends at that line, you get one line of rhythm, one emphasis, but if it ends in the middle of the line, you get something else, the run-on lines, enjambment. All these are techniques of poetry. Oh, the sentences mean what they mean, but the fact that they're put together in a line gives another emphasis, the way it does in poetry. You have the two kinds of syntax, the line endings and the run-on line, and the regular syntax of the language. You can be saying a lot more in a short space" (160–61). What he says was his first such effort, "Three Heroines," was "easy to write" because the story "just fell into place," leaving him free "to work on the lines, working out the form." He began all his other stories of that same period in the seventies the same way, but he would give up the verse form if he found halfway through that the stories got too long or that he could not sustain the form because the line ends were "not significant" or "no longer functional." His "ideal in writing," he says, is "that each sentence should have an intrinsic interest, and then that it should have an interest in terms of the whole story," thereby providing in fiction the same satisfaction associated with poetry (161). "To me that's what's fun about writing," he says. "It's like saying that life makes sense! Pretending that the small diurnal things make sense! Which of course they don't" (166).

Even if he does not completely realize this ideal in a given story, Taylor seems to find the playful exercise of striving for it both fun for the writer and beneficial at least in some lesser ways to the story's overall artistry. He does not make pretentious claims for his broken-line prose. "I don't call it free verse because it's not free verse," he says. "It's not that strict" (qtd. in Daniel 45). Robert Wilson reports hearing Taylor "tell an audience in jest that his stories turn out as stoems because he likes to lie on his back on a couch when he writes, holding above him the thin, spiral-bound notebooks in which he composes. 'They bend, you see, when I get to the middle of a line. So I just go and start another line' " ([iv]).

The very tone of this anecdote shows how Taylor refuses to take his techniques or his philosophy of composition too seriously. First and foremost, he seems to think, writing should be a joy. "I think it shows if a writer hasn't had fun, if he hasn't been excited by it and gotten ideas as he goes along," he told Ruth Dean. "Through writing, you learn what you think" (33).

That's one side of Taylor's poetics: the belief in writing as a high species of personal pleasure in which the spirit of creative play is paramount. The other side is much more serious but in no way incompatible with the first: the belief in writing as a hierophantic act that brings the writer and the reader in touch with the numinous. "I think I write because I have to write out of a compulsion and not because I have to turn out a book every year," he has told James Curry Robison. "I write because I get pleasure—and great pain too, though. But then I write to discover what I mean and out of necessity. It's more like a religious experience than like a professional experience. . . . I think if you're inspired by things coming together, interpreting some part of life, I think that's [what's important]" (138). To interviewer Barbara Thompson he similarly professes the conviction that "trying to write is a religious exercise" aimed at the understanding of life: "When I create, when I put my own mark on something and form it, I begin to know the whole truth about it, how it was put together. Then you can begin to change things around. You know all this after you have written a lot. You really know. And it has become the most important thing in your life. It has nothing to do with craft, or even art, in a way. It is making sense of life. It is coming to understand yourself" (158–59). Later in the same interview, Taylor once again denies that literary endeavor is adequately described by the term "profession": "I think that being a writer is much more the pursuit of a religion. . . . It's not a priesthood, but it's [only] one step back" (173).

The sacred object of this quasi-priestly vocation, then, is something ineffable and enigmatic. As he put it in his *Literature, Sewanee, and the World* address, "nearly everything about art is a mystery and must ever be so" ([3]).

What is remarkable is how much insight into this mystery he has been able to garner for himself and to share with his readers. In a tribute he wrote in 1985 for a University of Virginia Alderman Library chapbook on *The Fugitives, the Agrarians, and Other Twentieth Century Southern Writers,* Taylor tells how lucky he feels "to have grown up and come of age as a writer . . . where and when so many good and great writers were on the immediate landscape"—referring especially to John Crowe Ransom, Allen Tate, Robert Penn Warren, Cleanth Brooks, Donald Davidson, Andrew Lytle, and Katherine Anne Porter. With loving nostalgia he describes the "discourse at table" he and Robert Lowell enjoyed in such company. "There was talk," he recalls, "about literary matters and, it seems to me now, about all other matters. . . . For ourselves, I will say only this much, that we were sharp enough to see that we must learn from them. I don't know whether we learned more about how to write or how to live" ("Reminiscences" 20–21).

Peter Taylor's literary work—from *A Long Fourth* to *The Oracle at Stoneleigh Court*—leaves no doubt that he was an apt student who, at his masters' table or elsewhere, learned to probe the most subtle and mysterious aspects of life and art.

What has perhaps been less obvious to his general public is that the youth who originally disdained criticism has over the years himself become—like his mentors Ransom, Tate, Warren, and Brooks before him—a teacher and a theorist with a reasonably comprehensive, coherent, and consistent aesthetic that he not only embodies in his own work but also willingly and generously imparts to others. The scraps of discourse provided at Peter Taylor's table may well prove as invigorating and inspirational to the next generation (at least those who are "sharp enough" to see that they must learn from him) as the discourse of the preceding generation proved to him.

Locations Within Locations

ELIZABETH HARDWICK

I HAVE BEEN reading and rereading the Peter Taylor stories and novels since they started appearing in the 1940s. I remember them with some accuracy, if there can be an accurate memory of fiction. Every English or literature teacher knows the class cannot be summoned until the work, taught and read again and again, is read one more time on the brink of discussion. It's all in the details; a cliché, but then a phrase cannot be a cliché without having some truth in it.

Peter Taylor has had an exemplary career, and when we have at hand a product of his imagination, we always receive what we expect from having known the preceding work: high craftsmanship, purity of intention, perfect execution. He's a subtle writer in spite of the more or less frank clarity of his exposition, the way he tells the reader what is to be thought about the characters and the landscape in which the action takes place. On the other hand, there is a subterranean flow of ambiguity, complication, and mystery. Almost all of his characters, no matter how assertive, will wonder about themselves. In that way they have a kind of modesty—an odd trait on the contemporary scene where a blustering paranoia is so often the mark of personality.

There are some accents and stresses in the poetic sense that appear in the work as one begins to think about it in a general way. I suppose he is a "Southern" writer, although I wonder if that is strongly defining in Peter Taylor's work. He's certainly a writer of location, and his location is the Upper South of Tennessee, the towns of Nashville and Memphis and sometimes on up to St. Louis and sometimes backward glancing to Thornton, the imaginary rural place from which his black and white characters came to the city. The towns are a wide location with their resonant names, Nashville inland and Memphis spread out along the Mississippi River. More interesting to me are the thoughts about location within the location, that is, with the particular streets and what residence on them may indicate, the sections of the town, and who lives on what street, in what kind of house, and what street they may move along to or move up to or down to. This is a wonderful peculiarity in Taylor's use of setting. I myself am from a town in the Upper South, a town with pretensions sometimes tiresome, like his Nashville—my own town being Lexington, Kentucky. I know how *defining* placement can be, how subtle, and no one as far as I am aware has used this location within the location as tellingly as Peter Taylor. It is not simply the "wrong side of the tracks" or the "good part of town." It is also the magic of street names quite equal to the glow or lack of it in the family name.

In Taylor's fine early story, "Promise of Rain," a father is anxious about just what his sixteen-year-old son is doing with his time—the details of his "hanging out," as it would be referred to now. The father sees his son on Division Boulevard, and we are given a sort of archaeology of the street; then as we move along the father comes to Singleton Heights!, the exclamation point indicating, This is it!

Singleton Heights is an accomplishment, a definition of both obvious and obscure portent. "Great stucco and stone houses and white-washed brick—lawns are really meadows." The father leads us on with his entranced local mapmaking, which of course is not just territorial but carries a heavier weight of moral and especially social signification, or perhaps we should say *class* distinction. *Class,* a rather dangerous word threatening to go off like a gunshot, is not entirely suitable to Peter Taylor's imaginative placements. They have instead a dreamlike quality that reminds me somewhat of F. Scott Fitzgerald. The father goes on his way: "My own house, for instance, is in one of the gated-off streets that were laid out just north of Lawton Park at the turn of the century" (*HF* 47).

In "A Long Fourth," as we are being introduced to the cast and to the landscape, we learn that the home of the family is "eight miles from downtown Nashville on the Franklin Pike" (*LF* 140). Such are the details of authorial visualization; when extracted they may not be particularly arresting to the reader, but such offhand geography, dotted along the pages, translates from author to reader a very useful sense of intimacy, of being there.

Peter Taylor is a sort of casual historian of the middle-sized cities of the Upper South—Memphis, Nashville, and St. Louis. He has made his municipalities his own, laid them out psychologically like a surveyor putting orange ribbons on tree branches to mark the spaces and contours. The middle-sized city is still a community and strikingly so for those with youthful memories of the corner, the left-hand and right-hand swervings that will lead to the inner-communities, which are, if I read him correctly, his principal interest.

The Taylor cities are big enough to have a country club and, if my memory serves, large enough to have two country clubs and probably three nowadays. Indeed, there need to be at least two clubs for one of them to claim distinction as social award.

In the wonderful story "The Old Forest," the MCC (Memphis Country Club) and the Junior League, another middle-sized city institution (the home for unwayward girls, some used to call it), define the young woman Caroline.

Peter Taylor's stories bring personal anecdotes to mind. Just recently, I asked a friend from Shaker Heights, Ohio, about her sisters; she said one had a degree from Harvard Law School and the other was, well, a Junior Leaguer. So, Caroline is MCC and Junior League, but Lee Ann, the temptress, lives in a downtown rooming house, and for some reason she and her kind are called "city girls." I suppose that phrase is meant to indicate that the girls have no ancestral roots in an old country place, such as Thornton. We might note in the story that Caroline, through experience and moral questioning, advances, as it were, from the MCC to become a quite recognizable faculty wife—a bit of spiritual progress, if perhaps somewhat less fun.

"The Old Forest," with its gripping central plot situation, is, most would certainly agree, a triumph and a glittering ornament in the span of the American short story. Its melancholy and ruminating tone, its psychological refinement and sympathy cover the scene in a benign mist. And it preserves a special truthfulness about the not very remote conditions of life for the young: the fear of the disgrace of the broken engagement, the drama and trauma of it, not to mention the chaste engagement itself. We remember the rigidities of placement that would make certain quite ordinary and acceptable girls of the town seem out of bounds and therefore mysterious and tempting for a genteel young man.

There is a car accident, one of those troublesome, if not serious, happenings when a young man engaged to a suitable girl is out with another girl, a circumstance that might cause a driver's attention to wander. But it is Lee Ann who runs away, avoiding publicity, and the search for her, the questioning of her friends and landlady, gives the story its moral and emotional depth. And it all takes place in one of those magical town landmarks, the old forest, "a densely wooded area which is actually the last surviving bit of the primeval forest that once grew right up to the bluffs above the Mississippi River. Here are giant oak and yellow poplar trees older than the memory of the earliest white settler. Some of them surely may have been mature trees when Hernando de Soto passed this way, and were very old trees indeed when General Jackson, General Winchester, and Judge John Overton purchased this land and laid out the city of Memphis" (*OF* 38).

A Summons to Memphis is from beginning to end a father's story, even though it is narrated by a son who is forty-nine or so when the father is in his eighties. Fathers will surprise their children by unaccountable reversals of expectation, but they are still in this fiction old-fashioned men of character. One of the most striking scenes in the book occurs when, toward the end, the odious Mr. Shackleford and the father meet again after many years. Shackleford had ruined the family's fortune by a sort of junk-bond deal and brought about the necessity for a move from Nashville to Memphis. Memphis does not come out very well in this pairing and, in fact, is seen by the family as a traumatic exile and displacement. The narrator's father has forbidden his children to speak the name of Lewis Shackleford (43). However, toward the end of the story, the two men meet suddenly in a restaurant, and the narration goes: "My father rose from the table, took two steps forward to meet him, and the two tall and still very straight old men threw their arms about each other in such an ardent embrace that I felt myself on the verge of bursting into tears" (190). This would seem to be the wisdom of men experienced in the vicissitudes of business; or perhaps it indicates the strength of friendships, however fractured, by those who are themselves now old. Memory takes precedent.

In the stories that look backward, the theme seems to be that the moral depth of the dramatic happenings of youth are not truly understood until one has known through a long and complicated life the meaning of human vulnerability. I would contrast this father domination in much of Taylor's fiction with the novels and short stories coming out currently. The memory of childhood and youth within the family is, of course, the very spine of fiction, and it is no less so in the work of the new writers on the scene. But in these latter fictions, the child will usually remember the profoundly disturbing unpredictability of the parents, the very visible chaos of their lives, which often casts a diminishing shadow on the basic conception of parent and child.

Again and again we find the parents willful and perplexed, unstable, scarcely able to meet the steady and questioning eyes of the children. Divorce, love affairs, disappearances, drastic changes in status and income take place, not over a long period, but between the time the child goes to bed and the time he or she wakes in the morning. Real life, perhaps. In Mona Simpson's novel, *Anywhere but Here,* the young girl is trailing along with her mother who is in pursuit of a man, a lover, someone. The daughter is hoping that when they get to California her divorced father will take her to Disneyland, something like that. The parents have a terrible tendency to disappoint, to be late, to have other plans, often simply to forget the most solemn, if somewhat boozy, promise.

In the gifted Richard Ford's recent novel, *Wildlife,* about a sixteen-year-old boy and his windblown parents, the opening line is: "In the fall of 1960, when I was sixteen and my father was for a time not working, my mother met a man named Warren Miller and fell in love with him" (1). In this abdication from traditional assumptions, the parents are apt to be mercurial, not quite honest, and certainly less strict than the children. The emotion this curious reversal arouses is one of pathos. The son or daughter looks back with fatigue and bewilderment. What will they do next?

Something like this happens in *A Summons to Memphis,* but it is noticeable that the father waits until he is widowed and in his eighties to assert his right to surprise and confound. At the death of his wife the old man takes to going to places called The Blue Moon, The Yellow Parrot, and The Red Lantern. And he states his determination to marry again, a fate prevented in a cruel fashion by his two middle-aged, unmarried daughters. The father's condition is why the serious, responsible son, forty-nine years old, has received "a summons to Memphis." By surreptitious intervention the sisters arrange for the poor old father, a sort of Tennessee King Lear, to get left at the altar, literally. There are practical dynastic reasons for children to scream with pain at the thought of an old patriarch's taking on a new wife, but here a bit of retroactive revenge plays its part. The father, in his proper parental days, had subtly prevented the marriage of the two daughters and had turned the son, the narrator, away from the girl he loved in his youth. Another instance of the passing of the old ways has to do with the broad strokes in which the middle-aged sisters are drawn. They are loud and aggressive and like to "pour" their rather too robust figures into the most girlish, up-to-date fashions and thus to display, more or less unconsciously, a distance from their imagination of themselves as obviously ladies of "good background."

In speaking of Peter Taylor as a "Southern" writer, I have wanted to stress the fact that his subject matter is so often that of the middle-sized city. This I think somewhat sets him apart from the tradition, the male part of it at least. There is in Taylor's work a looking back to the time when the mothers and fathers lived on the family rural estates, but that is a memory, sentimental as such are likely to be. I notice in the body of his work the absence of hog killings, drunken weekends hunting duck, even the milder contemplative fishing tale. For myself I have strong reason to doubt this author knows how to load a rifle, on the page or off. And I also note the absence of the grotesques, the hollow-legged Bible salesmen, the "good country people," the Snopeses, and even those relentlessly loquacious grand old ladies so richly present on the Southern fictional scene.

Peter Taylor's world is not rural—it is middle class, at least before middle class was used to describe anyone merely not destitute. Indeed, in his towns the families he writes about would be of the best standing, upper class perhaps. The fiction is about manners, ways of acting, conflicts of feeling, repressions, and expectations. His well-to-do people carry with them a good deal of the baggage of Deep South fiction, that is, black cooks and yardmen and certain ideas of what is done and not done in good families. The mothers have a nostalgic cast to their thoughts, to the old days on the family place, but they are nevertheless rooted in the world of professional men, lawyers, and so on.

Not many of the stories deal with race relations, and when they do the touch is light, seen in a drifting, understated confrontation. "A Long Fourth," a powerful World War II story, brings together the lady of the household and the black cook. Essentially the theme is the wish of the women to keep the young men with them, either out of the army and the threat of death or out of a new life elsewhere. We have a son in the white family and a nephew the black cook has raised. Each of the women is trapped in her interior fear of loss, but they do not understand that this is what they share: the same emotion, the same drama.

Peter Taylor's serene and confident command of his art can make these complicated creations appear effortless. Of course, no writing is effortless, and only the severest effort can make it appear so. A natural gift for style seems always at hand in his works, a gift for texture and tone, for the measuring and pacing of effects, the smoothness and aptness of language. There is an alertness to the tremblings of individual consciousness—and also of conscience, the onset of moral torment that is so often the intellectual structure that supports the action.

In some ways Taylor's short and long works can be classed as comedies. The lightness of touch and the lack of moral insistence show the reign of an undogmatic spirit. Taylor can be moral without moralizing, and those characters who do fall into a moralizing rhetoric will have to suffer the defeats of experience. The traditional ways of life and their charms and certainties are not proposed as anything beyond the given of particular lives, how one was brought up, the placement in the scheme of things. Traditionalism as I see it in these pages is partly habit and partly pretense. The characters are not narrow-minded, but they are on occasion narrow in what they know and value only from the absence of wide experience rather than from ethical torpor—some of them, of course, because no generalization is invariably true in such sensitive creations.

The pathos of an attachment to traditional ways is seen in the very moving early story "The Scoutmaster." Uncle Jake, who has suffered the death of his wife and then the death of his nineteen-year-old daughter, is kind and sentimental and inclined to need a reassuring vision of things, even in the midst of new and puzzling rearrangements among his relatives. His fulfillment, as it is called, is his Thursday night position as the head of a Scout troop. (The Scoutmaster, as an image, has undergone a rather drastic downgrading in society, even sometimes producing a sinister overtone in the manner of the "good ole boy," but none of that was true at the time.) Indeed, this is one of the saddest of all Peter Taylor's stories in its portrayal of the unreality of backward longings.

At the end we find Uncle Jake standing before the boys in his Scout uniform and delivering his sincere, heart-wrung message:

> In that cold, bare, bright room he was saying that it was our great misfortune to have been born in these latter days when the morals and manners of the country had been corrupted, born in a time when we could see upon the members of our own families . . . the effects of our failure to cling to the teachings and ways of our forefathers. And he was saying that it was our duty and great privilege, as Boy Scouts, to preserve these honorable things which were left from the golden days when a race of noble gentlemen and

gracious ladies inhabited the land of the South. He was saying that we must preserve them until one day we might stand with young men from all over the nation to demand a return to the old ways and the old teachings everywhere. (*LF* 30–31)

The folly of Uncle Jake and his message is portrayed with human sympathy; sentimental posturings are an aspect of character, not a polemical platform. The control in this short story is perfectly balanced, and anyone would sigh for Uncle Jake.

The middle-sized city in the stories and the novel has changed its shape. It will not be cut into the memory of the present generation, at least not in the same way. "Downtown" had its banks and its clothing shops, with their ratings based on who shopped where; it had Woolworth's, the movie house, the bright streets of an evening. Downtown now, if lively at all, has had need of restoration, restaurants with exposed brick walls and hanging baskets, pasta, and blackened fish. These are attractions citizens might welcome, but they do not replace the lost memory of the central location with its churches, the public library, a statue here and there, and the streets with the best old houses. Of course, I have not meant to suggest that streets are the subject matter of Peter Taylor's fiction; they are instead a special minute particular. The subject matter is the family and its stresses, the generations.

The movement from the old sites to the suburbs appears in one of Taylor's late works. In a story called "The Captain's Son," from *In the Miro District,* a young couple has moved on and we leave them drinking bourbon "out there on some godforsaken street in the flat and sun-baked and endlessly sprawling purlieus of Memphis" (36). Flat and sun-baked and endlessly sprawling . . .

The Agrarians
The Halcyon Kinship

WARD SCOTT

PERHAPS NO FINER illustration of the fictional process exists than in Peter Taylor's short stories. Born and reared in Tennessee, Peter Taylor grew up artistically at the knees of John Crowe Ransom and Ransom's associates among the Fugitives and the Agrarians. An examination of the relationship between the Agrarians' *I'll Take My Stand* and Peter Taylor's "What You Hear from 'Em?" reveals the philosophical, social, and historical context for Peter Taylor's fictional community, Thornton, Tennessee.

The archetypal conflict of "What You Hear from 'Em?" is written about in *I'll Take My Stand* as the battle between agrarianism and industrialism. When the nation was formed, the founding fathers, Thomas Jefferson in particular, envisioned the United States as a nation of people devoted primarily to making an agricultural living. Founded on agrarian principles, the country soon changed, however, as the Industrial Revolution reached the shores of America. For a while thereafter the South and the West remained agrarian, the North and the East industrial, and with the Mississippi running down the center of the continent, the dichotomy was advantageous to both sections for quite some time. But as the country grew, tensions increased, complicated by slavery, tariffs, states' rights, and other competing economic interests. Writing in *I'll Take My Stand*'s "The Irrepressible Conflict," Frank Lawrence Owsley explains:

> When the balance of power was destroyed by the rapid growth of the North, and the destruction of this balance was signalized in the election of Lincoln by a frankly sectional, hostile political party, the South, after a futile effort at obtaining a concession from Lincoln which would partly restore the balance of power, dissolved its partnership with the industrial north.
> This struggle between an agrarian and an industrial civilization, then, was the irrepressible conflict. (91)

The outcome of this irrepressible conflict decided the country's future, and the nation shifted to a uniform, "standardized society and government" (88). Abraham Lincoln, a Republican, presided over this schismatic period in the nation's history. Defeated, then further devastated by the "reconstruction" that followed Lincoln's death, the South withdrew into itself. With the North's victory, the wheels had been set in motion for the industrial "Juggernaut" to roll into the future (91). Not only did Lincoln free the slaves, but he also became associated with a time in the nation's history when the winds of technology were released to batter the agrarian lifestyle.

"What You Hear from 'Em?" protagonist Aunt Munsie, born into slavery, is an embodiment of what industrialism did to the agrarian lifestyle. While serving as a domestic for the Tolliver family, Aunt Munsie raised Thad and Will Tolliver in the days when Thornton, Tennessee, had few motorcars and a human being had as much right to be in the middle of the road as a motorcar did. Before the widespread use of the motorcar made possible the rearrangement of family and place, Aunt Munsie's presence was essential to the stability of the Tolliver family.

Secure then in a society whose structure made her life humane and dignified, Aunt Munsie comes to long for those days when people had "quality." Quality people owned land, raised their families on the land, died on the land. From this love of the land came the values of the community. To be rich then had little to do with the accumulation of money or the possession of material goods. To be rich then meant to be a family member living in the Tolliver house, or the Pettigru house, or the Johnston house, examples of the antebellum Victorian architecture symbolic for Aunt Munsie of the days when the generations of Cameron County counted for something.

But, as in every situation of change, some welcome it, some object to it. Aunt Munsie, steadfast in her reluctance to accept it for the better, finds herself increasingly surrounded by community members who hold the opposite view. Munsie's daughter Lucrecie, for example, welcomes change for the better. Unlike Munsie, who was raised by Quality people, Lucrecie was raised by Has-Been quality people. Has-Been quality people are becoming the dominant class of citizens in Thornton. Together with a third class, people Munsie simply refers to as the Others, the Has-Beens are shiftless people who do not count for anything.

In effect, the dynamics behind the forces at work in Thornton are described by John Crowe Ransom in his contribution to *I'll Take My Stand.* Writing in "Reconstructed But Unregenerate," Ransom declared that "the generations following the industrial victory of the North had come to worship a religion called 'Progress' " (8). Furthermore, Ransom wrote that the worship of this religion had created what he termed the Modern Adam and Eve (7, 9). In Ransom's analysis, the first of two cornerstone analogies in *I'll Take My Stand,* the Modern Adam and Eve give their lives to the manufacture and acquisition of products made from nature's resources. According to Ransom, "Progress never defines its ultimate objective, but thrusts its victims at once into an infinite series" (8). Therefore, Adam and Eve's production and acquisition of products and the energy they put into that production and acquisition are endless. Living as if there is no end in sight to the energy he can pour into his dominion over nature, Adam pursues everything he does with the aim of helping himself do his job more efficiently. His Protestant work ethic ensures that his worship of progress is done with the proper attitude, and should he occasionally become lackadaisical, Eve, who also worships the Gospel of Service, ensures that he never loses sight of the fact that his manufacture and acquisition of products should not fall behind that of the next Adam down the block (10). Should his energies flag, Adam would be less than a productive member of society. Thus his "whole duty" as a man would be detrimental to "the gross material prosperity" of the culture at large. The measure of Adam is the measure of his culture, and the measure of his culture is directly proportional to the volume of Adam's "material production" (12).

It is this progressive mind-set that dominates the town of Thornton at the time of Aunt Munsie's dilemma. Tugging a slop wagon through the Thornton streets, Aunt Munsie no longer occupies the station in life she once did when her word was law in the Tolliver household. As her story unfolds, societal pressures increase to have her removed from the city streets. As the story closes, ordinances have been passed and Aunt Munsie's pigs are sold to Herb Mallory, who lives beyond the city limits. Through the use of the slop wagon, Peter Taylor makes specific these community pressures. In fiction, change never occurs abstractly; one behavior plays itself against another. Caught in a world that decreasingly tolerates farm animals in town, Aunt Munsie and her slop wagon, "a long, low, four-wheeled vehicle about the size and shape of a coffin, paraded down the center of the street without any regard for, if with any awareness of, the traffic problems she sometimes made" (CS 236), reduce to an image the conflict discussed in *I'll Take My Stand*.

Good fiction derives its tension from the reader's growing concern over how the protagonist will resolve her dilemma and how this resolution will affect the protagonist's life. Once upon a time, when Aunt Munsie had as much right to be on a street as an automobile, a "vehicle was a vehicle, and a person was a person, each with the right to move as slowly as he pleased and to stop where and as often as he pleased" (237). But people in Thornton are not as polite and as respectful of each other as they used to be. Old Mr. Hadley hurries about in his Mama's coupe, tooting the insignificant little horn and "shouting at Aunt Munsie in his own tooty voice" (242). The new generation of high school kids is equated with Yankee strangers in its propensity for impoliteness. The town's manners decline. The decline finds focus in Aunt Munsie's dilemma. Aunt Munsie, a holdover from an agrarian era when almost everyone in town kept animals, cannot keep pace. People less and less keep pigs in their yards and more and more rely on the Piggly Wiggly chain grocery store for their mass-produced food. Parents of the rude high school boys no longer look to the land for their source of wealth but work instead in "the five-and-ten cent store" where Adam's standardized products are cheaply sold. Still other parents—those Lucrecie no doubt thinks of as "white trash" (for she has been raised by the Has-Been middle-class whites)—work at the mill or in "factory town," establishments owned by Yankee outsiders who have little respect for agrarian traditions (240, 238).

Allen Tate, in his "Remarks on Southern Religion," wrote of the spiritual price Adam was going to have to pay for worshiping the Gospel of Progress. In what amounts to the thesis of *I'll Take My Stand,* Tate reasoned that "abstraction is the death of religion no less than the death of anything else" (156). In the second of the two cornerstone *I'll Take My Stand* analogies, in a comparison he terms the metaphor of "The Whole Horse," Tate explains how Modern Adam will become hopelessly locked into his progressive frame of mind. Because Adam's mind-set will allow him to believe he can dominate nature, Adam's perception of nature will be affected. When he looks at a whole horse, for example, Adam will not be able to see a whole horse. He will only be able to see "half of the horse—that half which may become a dynamo, or an automobile, or any other horsepowered machine" (157). A truly religious mind, Tate wrote, "is concerned with the whole horse . . . and not with . . . that power of the horse which he shares with horsepower in general, of pushing or pulling another object" (156–57).

But Adam will not have a truly religious mind. Adam's mind will be "abstract and scientific" (157). Adam will focus only on that which is tolerable to his rational mind. The whole horse will not be tolerable to Adam's rational mind because Adam cannot always dominate the whole horse. The whole horse is a flesh-and-blood horse, and there may be days when the flesh-and-blood horse does not feel like working. A mechanical horse will always work, however, as long as there is gas and oil to fuel its engine. And Adam can supply those. Adam can exert his will on the half a horse. The half a horse, the half Adam identifies with horsepower, is workable. The workable is tolerable to the progressive mind. The workable is logical; the whole horse is illogical. But the whole horse is alive, breathing, aging, dying. The whole horse is natural. So Adam will rely on the machine because the machine is more efficient, more productive. However, in relying on the machine rather than the horse, Adam will lose his true spirituality, for a truly religious person does not reduce the world to the workable, the practical. The truly religious person accepts the "horse as he is" (157). He does not accept the horse on the condition that the horse first conform to the demands of some special requirement.

Aunt Munsie's problem—that she does not want the world she loves to change—is complicated by the fact that the very children she holds so dear, and who in turn hold her dear, have left Thornton to become members of the half-a-horse mentality. Feigning deafness to block out what she does not want to hear, Aunt Munsie uses the phrase "What You Hear from 'Em?" to show her obsession with the return of the Tolliver children.

But Thad and Will are rich by Miss Lucille Satterfield's criterion. One day Miss Lucille, the Modern Eve, the embodiment of Thornton's emerging status quo, the "daughter, wife, sister, mother of lawyers," presents Aunt Munsie with this modern definition of prosperity: "They're *all* prospering so, Munsie. Mine *and* yours. You ought to go down to Memphis to see them now and then, the way I do. Or go up to Nashville to see Mr. Will. I understand he's got an even finer establishment than Thad" (241). Aunt Munsie in reply can only drop "the tongue of her wagon noisily on the pavement" (241–42). In an action, the old way of life clatters against the new. Aunt Munsie's dismay at Miss Lucille Satterfield's suggestion implies the universal significance of Munsie's conflict with the old and the new. The departed Tolliver boys, in seeking their fortunes as young men do, left Thornton to own Ford and Lincoln automobile franchises in Memphis and Nashville. Lincoln, the Republican, the victorious leader of the industrial North, helped set in motion the forces that eventuate the social phenomenon spearheaded by Henry Ford. Shortly after the turn of the century, when Aunt Munsie would have been somewhere in her fifties, Henry Ford's assembly line ushered in industrial technology at a new standard of efficiency. This new standard of efficiency helped provide Miss Lucille Satterfield with her new definition of prosperity.

But for Munsie, the real source of wealth is love born out of family. Aunt Munsie regards those days when the Tollivers were young and she was their surrogate mother as "halcyon days" (244). (The word is the storyteller's, but the memory is Munsie's.) Families stayed closer to home then because travel was less efficient. The juxtaposition of *halcyon* with *Ford* and *Lincoln* suggests the complexities of Aunt Munsie's predicament, complexities that are echoed in the Ransom and Tate essays. The halcyon was a Greek mythological bird, usually a kingfisher, which built its nest on the sea and had the power to calm the waves. On land, man's forms have found their civilized apex. But these forms are always shifting: governments change, countries change, even philosophical viewpoints change. The kingfisher nest floated on the sea. To early civilized man, this kinship must have appeared perfect, for what more stable relationship could a creature enjoy than to be at rest in the ceaseless movement of the sea? Reasoning therefore out of knowledge archetypal, Aunt Munsie believes that Thad and Will's return will resume her halcyon days and thus the halcyon days for all those who believe in the old way of life based on agrarian traditions.

But what the reader realizes early, Aunt Munsie will not accept until the very end: Thad and Will are never going to return permanently to Thornton. As a resolution for Aunt Munsie's predicament, and consequently the town's, the two boys (it matters not to Aunt Munsie which one it was) engineer the mechanism that makes possible Aunt Munsie's final removal as an obstacle to progress. Because many citizens of Thornton retain a lingering sense of loss for the mannerly agrarian traditions that structured their formative years and because paradoxically the loss of those traditions has placed Munsie's life in danger, the conspiracy to remove Aunt Munsie from the city streets is accomplished as gently as possible. That the city fathers look to Thad and Will for assistance in removing Aunt Munsie from the streets demonstrates the residual effects of community influence born from historic connections. The women have tried to remove Munsie, but the mayor's office no longer listens to women. On 26 August 1920 women had been given the right to vote, largely as a result of their work in factories alongside men during the Great War. In an irony that foreshadows the perils of the new, the women, standardized by their political freedoms, no longer have personal influence in community government.

But Thad Tolliver, who had nearly gone "crazy when he heard their old house had burned" (238) and had once threatened to sue the town for not protecting the past by caring for the old Victorian houses (houses named in yet another irony after Queen Victoria's age, which earmarked the beginnings of the Industrial Revolution in England), still has the influence necessary to "set the wheels of the conspiracy in motion" (246). Operating not as an official of the town but as a concerned human being, Thad resolves Aunt Munsie's dilemma once and for all. If there are no longer pigs in Thornton, there can no longer be a need for an Aunt Munsie to slop them. And the need for everyone to keep pigs in town has diminished as the number of Piggly Wigglys throughout the South has increased. The reader knows by now that the number will not soon decrease because more roads are being built down which travel more trucks, built in more factories, bringing more produce and staples from an expanding, corporate community.

Aunt Munsie's fight is over when the edict is passed that no one can any longer keep pigs in Thornton. Because progress has reduced the number who still do keep pigs to two, the decree's results mark the end of a particular form of social order. In a dramatic moment, Aunt Munsie confronts the constable who himself has been one of the remaining two pig keepers. Aunt Munsie, whose word had once been "law," and the sheriff, whose word is currently law, are guilty of the same violation (244). Out of respect for Aunt Munsie's dignity as a human being, the town applies the law equally to both. Thus the community, with its roots in the agrarian past, shares the application of justice and tempers it with love. Possible only in a society where there exists a common heritage, this polite and personal application of justice softens the blow for Munsie and renders the humanity of the town.

"Slavery," John Crowe Ransom wrote, "was a feature monstrous enough in theory, but, more often than not, humane in practice" (14). The town respects Aunt Munsie because she was once a surrogate mother for Thad and Will Tolliver. That Thad and Will view Munsie, a former slave, as a member of their family is different from the way the Has-Been whites view Lucrecie. "It was because while Aunt Munsie had been raising a family of white children, a different sort of white people from hers had been raising her own child, Crecie" (240). Indeed, "Mr. Thad and Mr. Will had bought Munsie her house, and Crecie had heired hers from her second husband" (244). Even the "porch banisters and pillars had come off a porch of the house where [Thad and Will] had grown up" (234). Dr. Tolliver, "with a special eye for style and for keeping up with the times" (236), had unintentionally contributed to the demise of Munsie's preferred way of life when he removed some of the Victorian symbols from his house, but in an action that shows the paradoxical effects of change, Aunt Munsie helps sustain that preferred way when she uses Dr. Tolliver's discarded parts to enhance her own home.

"What industrialism counts as goods and riches of the earth the agrarian South does not, nor ever did," wrote Andrew Lytle in *I'll Take My Stand*'s "The Hind Tit" (208). Aunt Munsie, Thad and Will's surrogate mother, once did her work in terms of the land, thereby deriving spiritual values from that special relationship with the planter society that viewed nature as the whole horse and not the half a horse. Zinnias and cannas and even the wandering Jew, potted in a rusty lard bucket, have a home in Munsie's yard. Lard, the rendered fat of hogs that Munsie keeps in her yard, finds yet another use in that its container, weathered by nature, makes a home for flowers named after a nomadic people whose wanderings are not dissimilar in many ways from the wanderings of both Aunt Munsie and Thad and Will Tolliver.

But Aunt Munsie has tried to stop her wandering whereas Thad and Will have not. That Will and Thad recognize that they still have a need for the agrarian source of spiritual strength embodied in Munsie is a testimony to the spiritual deprivation of the modern world in which Thad and Will have most recently come to live. To ensure that their children know that spiritual strength of the agrarian world before it is all gone, Thad and Will continue to bring their children and their children's children to Thornton to be hugged by Aunt Munsie. Deracinated, Thad and Will even dream of returning to Thornton and buying a piece of property "a mile north of town" or "on the old River Road" and building themselves "a jim-dandy house there" (234). But their conversion to the urban life of the Modern Adam, the age of the half-a-horse mentality, prevents them from fulfilling their spiritual need.

The denouement of "What You Hear from 'Em?" arrives as Aunt Munsie realizes the ultimate consequences of the forces at work in Thornton. Until now, the tension has been building over how the heroine will resolve her growing awareness of these forces and how they will affect her life. Aunt Munsie has gone from a child born in Guinea, West Africa, to a slave to a surrogate mother to a slop wagon lady. In a final visionary glimpse, she discovers the shape of life to come.

"A collie dog's a collie dog anywhar," she tells her animals in a fit of newly acquired knowledge. "But Aunt Munsie, she's just their Aunt Munsie here in Thornton" (249). Because of Aunt Munsie's epiphany, the reader can now deduce the story's central statement: the nation is moving into an age wherein man's perception of his relationship to nature has been forever altered. As artificial, corporate human beings take charge of the earth, the flesh-and-blood people, their heritage fragmented by the abstractions of the half-horse mentality, become migrants wandering anonymously from city to city. *Abstraction is the death of religion no less than the death of anything else.* Aunt Munsie's keen insight illustrates the truth behind Allen Tate's thesis. Had Aunt Munsie moved to Nashville or Memphis because of the death of agrarianism, her community kinships, which are becoming more and more diffused even in Thornton, would have been even more depersonalized in those larger cities. A collie dog is a specific breed of dog known to have been bred for a particular purpose, no matter where it lives. But, unlike the collie dog, Aunt Munsie would lose her time-honored identity in Nashville or Memphis and consequently her individuality. In Thornton, where collective memory knows her as a person, she derives dignity from her past.

John Crowe Ransom, writing of the modern world, said, "It is out of fashion in these days to look backward rather than forward" (*I'll Take My Stand* 1). That Thad and Will look back to Thornton therefore differentiates them from the Has-Beens and the Others who have moved to town to operate the Piggly Wiggly. That Aunt Munsie comes to terms with the new order by claiming to remember "the day General N. B. Forrest rode into town and saved all the cotton from the Yankees at the depot" (250) demonstrates her halcyon moment. Old people tend to remember the best and forget the worst. In her final role as a member of the town square, she, along with "all the other old-timers," freezes change at the period in history she would most like change to stop (250).

Robert Penn Warren, writing in "The Briar Patch," his contribution to *I'll Take My Stand,* spoke of the Negro's frustration in finding a place for himself once the Civil War was over: "The Southern negro has always been a creature of the small town and farm. That is where he still chiefly belongs, by temperament and capacity; there he has less the character of a 'problem' and more the status of a human being who is likely to find in agricultural and domestic pursuits the happiness that his good nature and easy ways incline him to as an ordinary function of his being" (260). Criticized as having expressed an anachronistic view of blacks (surely the critics are modern Adams with the half-a-horse mentality), Warren might have explained his vision more clearly had he written, "The agrarians, both black and white, of the planter society have always been creatures of the small town and farm," for throughout the essays written by the various contributors to *I'll Take My Stand*, that theme runs continuously.

For example, writing in "The Philosophy of Progress," Lyle Lanier explained that "the only reality which is ultimately worth considering is that of human beings which associate together; and the life of the family is the life which actual fathers, mothers, and children live in one another's company. . . . And these benefits we are fast surrendering to the industrial order, whose patterns of conduct are incompatible with the conditions necessary to the stability and integrity of family life" (147).

Writing in "Education, Past and Present," John Gould Fletcher asserted, "We [Modern Adams] have a mental habit—not the least pernicious of all our habits—of regarding the savage races of mankind as rude and uncultivated, and of ourselves by contrast as 'civilized' and even 'progressive.' But a few hours of reading at anthropology suffices to dissipate the illusion that there are any races on the earth's surface so primitive as to lack all the elements of culture" (99).

In "Whither Southern Economy," Herman Clarence Nixon put the loss of agrarian influence in classical context: "Southerners in strategic or public position should take warning against the evils of a discriminatory encouragement of rapid industrialization in their section. They can profit by recalling that the decline of the Roman Empire was accompanied by the neglect of agriculture and the growth of an idle urban proletariat of unwieldy proportions" (195–96).

Even in "A Mirror For Artists," Donald Davidson noted: "More completely, the making of an industrialized society will extinguish the meaning of the arts, as humanity has known them in the past, by changing the conditions of life that have given art a meaning. For they have been produced in societies which were for the most part stable, religious, and agrarian; where the goodness of life was measured by a scale of values having little to do with the material values of industrialism; where men were never too far removed from nature to forget that the chief subject of art, in the final sense, is nature" (29).

Longing for a resolution to the dilemma caused by the outcome of the irrepressible conflict, John Crowe Ransom could only hope that the Democratic Party would hold to "agrarian, conservative, anti-industrial" principles so that those who loved the land could offer an alternative voice in the Republic's government (26). In a further attempt to provide the country with a method for a balanced way of life, Lyle Lanier hoped that the nation would try "to effect a synthesis of the unified manner of living inherent in the agrarian family and community with the energy and inventiveness which have been diverted into industrialism" (154). Regardless of the particular suggestion each contributor made, *I'll Take My Stand* essayists collectively worried that the nation would become an imbalanced society of experts who had little identity as human beings.

Certainly "What You Hear from 'Em?" renders in a particular sense of place and carefully selected details the rich and complicated concerns of *I'll Take My Stand*. Using the town bard whose omniscient sensibilities neither defend nor attack the old or the new way of life, Peter Taylor reveals that Aunt Munsie suffers what is perhaps the most universal of all human longings: the heartfelt need to arrest change when the inherent social order is most pleasing to her. Tensions are never abstract in fiction. Aunt Munsie's subsequent search to fit in somewhere after her beloved way of life has been disrupted forms the enveloping action of "What You Hear from 'Em?" That the nuances and subtleties of the concretions that structure Peter Taylor's short story are well codified in a collection of essays his fellow Southerners once wrote does not, to be sure, make his work a product of *I'll Take My Stand*. Rather, the existence of the essays reveals Peter Taylor's artistic connections to a remarkable group of visionary people who found themselves yearning for their halcyon kinship.

As for Aunt Munsie (who is based on Peter Taylor's own mammy, Easter Sellers), the Tolliver children and their children's children continue to visit and to be hugged by her, but they never again set foot in her backyard once she sells her pigs. Unconcerned about the facts of her situation because she is helpless to do anything about them, Aunt Munsie lives on with heroic courage for some twenty years thereafter. But her spirit softens, and her memory dims to spare her heartache for her vanishing love.

Troubled Gardens

Peter Taylor's Pastoral Equations

CREIGHTON LINDSAY

CRITICS HAVE FOR some time addressed the opposition of city and rural life as a dominant theme in Peter Taylor's fiction. Albert Griffith, in early commentary, noted that Taylor often focuses on the manners of urban characters whose belief systems "relate back to the country town which anteceded them" (1970 ed. 157). In their persistent compulsion to gaze back, Taylor's characters tend to exhibit nostalgic paralysis or reluctant acceptance of change—willingly sharing epiphanies or proudly displaying obstinate myopia. Taylor's consistent juxtaposition of urban and country life places his work—at least tangentially—in the tradition of the American pastoral, a literary mode that probes—as Leo Marx has framed it—"what possible bearing . . . the urge to idealize a simple, rural environment [can] have upon the lives of men . . . in an intricately organized, urban, industrial, nuclear-armed society" (*Machine* 5). My purpose is to explore how Taylor's best fiction reveals him as a unique and important voice in the American pastoral tradition.

Defining "pastoral," however, is not a simple task. The term has become—like "metaphor"—so inclusive as to suggest hopeless ambiguity—for, as Wayne Booth speculates about the latter, "any word that means everything can only mean nothing" (303). It is not my concern here to attempt a definitive understanding of the term, nor do I have the space to review the rich scholarship having to do with this ancient tradition, but I do believe it is possible to establish a working understanding that will allow for a productive examination of Taylor's fiction.

In its "loose sense," as Lawrence Buell writes, pastoral literature is "preoccupied with nature and rurality as setting, theme, and value in contradistinction from society and the urban" (1). The natural world is an ideal that the urban individual seeks as refuge from the dispiriting and psychologically fractious quality of social and cultural reality. In its traditional, premodern sense, the pastoral landscape was recognized as essentially idyllic, often posited as overtly mythic and unattainable, and characteristically represented in intrinsically human settings—orchards, gardens, shepherds' fields. In this tradition, the pastoral sense of place functions in an essentially figurative way—always as a self-conscious metaphor for the Edenic perfect place. Early scholarship on the American pastoral suggested that one difference between it and its European precursors was a sense that the American landscape was somehow less figurative, offering an authentic "place apart, secluded from the world—a peaceful, lovely, classless, bountiful pasture" (Marx, *Machine* 116). In this view of the mode, the self-consciousness of the figure is attenuated; the American pastoral landscape is represented and perceived as idyllic yet somehow attainable in the real world. Much recent scholarship on the subject of the American pastoral has tended to focus on this "literalization" of the landscape in American narrative, tracing it and challenging its assumptions in a variety of ways. The burden of suspicion placed on the American pastoral has resulted in a tendency by some scholars to dismiss the mode as arcane at best or inane at worst.

Yet recently a number of critics have come to the tradition's defense. Leo Marx, in reassessing some of his earlier views, suggests that "pastoralism, so far from being an anachronism in the era of high technology, may be suited to the ideological needs of a large, educated, relatively affluent, mobile, yet morally and spiritually troubled segment of the white middle class" ("Pastoralism" 40). Glen Love, echoing Marx, insists that "reports of pastoralism's demise have proven premature" (195). Although Lawrence Buell admits that American pastoral's ideological motifs are "too complex to permit monolithic categorization" (5), he also maintains that "pastoral ideology is a powerful lens through which to see our literary culture" (21). Having admitted the difficulty of unifying pastoral theory, Buell comes surprisingly close to articulating just such a monolithic way of viewing the mode when he describes its essentially dichotomous nature, which he sees as "built into American pastoral thinking from the start, for it was conceived as a dream both hostile to the standing order of civilization (decadent Europe, later hypercivilizing America) yet at the same time a model for the civilization in the process of being built. So American pastoral was always both counterinstitutional and institutionally sponsored" (20). For Buell, the fact that American pastoral ideology has always been a "target moving in two directions at once" (20) is grounds for eager inquiry rather than frustrated dismissal.

Peter Taylor's pastoral is enigmatic in just the dichotomous way Buell sees as fundamental to American pastoralism. Taylor's narrators frequently seem unaware of the contradiction between their nostalgia for an idealized, rural past on the one hand and their wholehearted embrace of urban opportunity on the other. Although theme often issues from this contradiction, narrative momentum thrives in the unawareness with which it is divulged. There is, for example, a revealing yet elusive inconsistency in the way Phillip Carver, the narrator of *A Summons to Memphis,* comments in seemingly dispassionate terms on how his father's willfulness prevented an opportunity to spend a night at the old family homestead in Thornton during the family move from

Nashville to Memphis. Phillip—who has himself escaped from "rural" Memphis to life in New York City—presents the moment as a missed opportunity and in doing so betrays a wistfulness about a pastoral better place, describing it as a "retreat from the world" (35). Phillip's withdrawal to New York is thus a retreat from a retreat and captures the duality described in Buell's description of American pastoralism.

Another Taylor character who embodies Buell's sense of the duality of American pastoral thinking is Quintus Cincinnatus Lovell Dudley, in *A Woman of Means,* who is caught between his maternal grandmother's rural values and his father's urban aspirations. Quintus seems stuck in a paradoxical middle ground where city and country need each other to define the other's limitations and advantages. As he gradually overcomes his insecurities and gains self-confidence among his family and schoolmates in the sophisticated and urbane world of St. Louis, where his father has remarried and resettled, Quintus is haunted by memories of his grandmother's farm in Tennessee, where he had spent summers before moving permanently to St. Louis. Quintus typically indulges in his retrospective reveries about the farm when he feels most threatened by his new life in the city, yet the farm of his memories is not without the troubling imprint of civilization: grim reminders of the Civil War, an "ancient hitching ring in the side of a giant oak" (47), his grandfather's abandoned and disintegrating old brick office.

It is important to bear in mind that Taylor does not frame his fictions in overtly pastoral settings. Writers who often do so—Willa Cather, James Fenimore Cooper, John Steinbeck—tend to make pastoral motifs the very fabric of their narratives. Cather's prairie novels, for example, explore the tensions between revered past and troubled present in a setting—America's developing agricultural heartland—that is intrinsically pastoral. Taylor, on the other hand, tends to be more furtive in his approach to pastoral concerns. Certainly the bulk of Taylor's narratives deal in some way with the dynamics between past and present, city and country. But these dynamics in and of themselves do not make for a pastoral mode. Linked to the disjunctions of time and place must be the sense that the present and the urban are too heavily laden by civilization and technology; the past, which connotes the simpler life of the garden, must be examined as an alternative. Taylor's pastoral vision typically occurs in condensed, concentrated, and often highly metaphoric instances within the larger frame of the narrative. These "pastoral insets," as Andrew Ettin calls them, "place a small pastoral moment or scene within a larger, nonpastoral context" (81). Although Taylor's stories rarely take place in pastoral settings, the garden is never far from the narrative frame. Once the pastoral inset has been introduced, it imbues the fiction with its presence and makes the tension between past and present—country and city—a motif to be reckoned with.

Examples of pastoral insets in Taylor's fiction are legion. In "A Spinster's Tale," for example, Elizabeth recalls retreating fleetingly from the oppressive sadness of her mother's sickroom by focusing on the world of nature: "Outside it was spring. The furnishings of the great blue room seemed to partake for that one moment of nature's life" (*CS* 144). In this example, nature and human landscape come together as a liminal space for Elizabeth, mediating between the passing innocence of youth and the troubled future that will follow her mother's death. In traditional pastoral fashion, nature here is posited as a therapeutic refuge, and Elizabeth appears to recognize it as such. Most of Taylor's pastoral insets, however, are not so straightforward. And it is in his ability to tease the mode, to vary its role in constructing a narrative's particular moral and ideological center, that Taylor proves himself a master of using the pastoral—in Buell's sense—as a moving target.

Taylor's tendency to probe the limits of the pastoral tradition sets him apart from a variety of Southern writers who have typically represented the South either as Arcadia realized or as a site in which to regain a temporarily lost pastoral garden. Lucinda Hardwick MacKethan has suggested that writers like Thomas Nelson Page, Joel Chandler Harris, Jean Toomer, and William Faulkner frequently exhibit a trust in the pastoral impulse that comes "from unquestioning faith or private preference rather than any reasoned exploration or objective perception of the ideal itself as it relates to their images of the South" (3). Taylor demonstrates no such "unquestioning faith." Although he certainly positions himself on one level as a "Southern writer" through his consistent exploration of the South as setting and state of mind, his pastoral insets never reveal an ideology that sets the South apart as a site of actual or potential pastoral perfection. If Peter Taylor has a "private preference," it is for the South as a fascinating source of interesting fictional representation rather than as a discrete pastoral territory.

Frequently, Taylor's pastoral insets reveal characters whose understanding of, or regard for, nature is either so superficial or deficient that the traditional role of the pastoral landscape as the place of refuge gets thrown into question. In what we have come to think of as the conventional American pastoral inset, the point at which the protagonist meditates on nature is typically a vortex of important personal growth. The pastoral landscape often serves as a kind of catalyst for understanding, allowing the protagonist to sort out some or all of the conflicts framed by the narrative. This curative process frequently occurs because the pastoral landscape functions as a kind of profound reminder of human unity with grand, inscrutable, and transcendent nature. Early in Cather's *My Antonia,* for example, Jim Burden recalls an epiphanic moment that occurs not long after his arrival at his grandparents' Nebraska farm. Burden, left alone in the garden, sits among the pumpkins and meditates on a vague sense of contentment inspired by nature's apparent uneventfulness:

"Nothing happened. I did not expect anything to happen. I was something that lay under the sun and felt it, like the pumpkins, and I did not want to be anything more. I was entirely happy" (14). Burden, in his retrospective interpretation of this moment, suggests that he had been "dissolved into something complete and great" (14). Taylor's characters, by contrast, often find themselves alienated by their own perplexity regarding nature. During a pivotal scene in "The Other Times," the protagonist pauses to look at the night sky and notes that it was "like an old, washed-out gray sweater" (*CS* 94). Rather than feeling refreshed or reminded of nature's healthy presence, the protagonist moves out of the pastoral inset with the sense that the world—even the natural world—is "ugly and raw" (94). When Taylor's narrators are unreliable—as in "The Other Times"—they cause us to mistrust their assessments of these pastoral moments. In effect, we wish that they would take the opportunity—like Cather's Jim Burden—to dissolve into "something complete and great," and the fact that they miss such opportunities is frequently one of Taylor's clearest signals that we should not completely trust them.

When Taylor's protagonists fail to seize the pastoral moment or otherwise demonstrate alienation from the pastoral landscape, they expand the way the pastoral conventionally operates in narratives. Nature, in fact, sometimes recedes in importance in Taylor's pastoral vision to such an extent that it becomes replaced by mere escapism as the guiding narrative impulse, an impulse Renato Poggioli identifies as central to the "urban" pastoral, which "transplant[s] the pastoral yearning for a solitary independence, for the self-sufficiency of a purely private life, from the open spaces of the countryside to a secluded corner or cell-like enclosure" (33). In one sense, the notion of Taylor as a master of the "urban pastoral" is attractive given the number of characters in Taylor's narratives, like Phillip Carver in *A Summons to Memphis,* who seem so utterly lost in the world—including the world of nature—that they find their refuge in purely human artifacts: apartments, clothes, family heirlooms. Yet even Phillip Carver must—from time to time—reckon with the natural landscape and its effect on him. His fondest memories are of the times he and his first love, Clara Price, sat contentedly together admiring a waterfall in front of Clara's house: "We delighted in it especially when there were inlets of ice along the edges, and the water flow seemed to have to make a great struggle not to freeze together" (95). Such a meditation comes close to inspiring the kind of transcendence experienced by Jim Burden in the pumpkin patch, except that we are disturbed by the fact that Phillip Carver never returns to such natural landscapes as sites of salvation. Instead, he quite consciously escapes from them to the refuge of his apartment in New York City. Arguably, Jim Burden is as unreliable a narrator as Phillip Carver, but the striking difference between them is that whereas Burden seems always aware of nature's potential and desires to recapture its palliative essence, Carver seems relentlessly determined to retreat from his waterfall in resentful and short-sighted denial. Poggioli maintains that the technique of "presenting a bucolic aspiration only to deny it" (34) constitutes an "inverted" pastoral, and he insists that such an inversion is "ironic and ambiguous, since it begins as imitation and ends as parody" (33). Certainly the disparity between what the characters often report and what the author and reader know to be true regarding the role of nature in Taylor's narratives is intrinsically ironic. Moreover, Taylor's nature is ambiguous in the way it functions both as an ideal and as an indicator of how characters have allowed the vicissitudes of life to dull their senses to the salutary power of nature *as* an ideal. But to suggest that Taylor's inverted pastoral is simple parody is to overlook the sophisticated and complex ways in which the inversion of the convention serves to comment on society. Whereas some of Taylor's characters fool themselves with the pastoral ideal, others miss the symptoms of a need for that ideal. In the end, although nature sometimes plays a subdued or inverted role in Taylor's pastoral vision, it is too prevalent and intricate a theme for us to cast him as mere urban pastoralist or simple parodist.

Taylor's consistent use of pastoral insets—both conventional and inverted—suggests a definitive stance toward nature. Taylor's nature may shift as a pastoral register, but behind its changing appearance is a consistent attitude regarding how humans might define their relationship to it. Such ideological positioning seems important given imminent ecological crisis, and Taylor's use of the pastoral—although not overtly concerned with a deteriorating environment—points to an agitated lack of confidence in human ability to understand or exist harmoniously with nature. One of the most explicit indications of Taylor's general alarm figures in the complex dynamics of the guiding metaphor in "The Old Forest"—the forest itself. The story's narrator, Nat Ramsey, offers a description of the stand of old growth trees that implies criticism of the way human proprietary instincts clash in the relatively neutral setting of the forest: "It is a grove, I believe, that men in Memphis have feared and wanted to destroy for a long time and whose destruction they are still working at even in this latter day. It has only recently been saved by a very narrow margin from a great highway that men wished to put through there—saved by groups of women determined to save this last bit of the old forest from the axes of modern men. Perhaps in old pioneer days, before the plantation and neoclassic towns were made, the great forests seemed woman's last refuge from the brute she lived alone with in the wilderness" (*OF* 53). Although it is important to bear in mind that this passage is Nat Ramsey's interpretation rather than Peter Taylor's polemic, it seems clear that the rhetoric of narrator, implied author, and career author appear to intersect. We may have our doubts about some aspects of Nat Ramsey's character, but his tone and diction in this passage suggest that he believes human insensitivity toward nature is not a good thing, and Peter Taylor would seem to want his reader to agree with Nat's critical stance. Clearly Nat wants his audience to perceive man's jealous and obsessive drive to conquer nature as untenable. Moreover, it seems reasonable to suggest that the heroic vitality in "The Old Forest" inheres in the engagement of its female characters—Lee Ann Deehart's drive to buck the rigid social system by fleeing into the old forest, Caroline Braxley's eventual management of the crisis that leads to the story's resolution. In Nat's description of the environmental crisis represented by the male instinct to control the natural environment, the women are again the heroic force, uniting to save nature from the "axes of modern men." In modern American culture, Taylor appears to be saying, the pastoral place of refuge is threatened.

As I have suggested, the "nature" of the pastoral traditionally has been the "nature" of the garden, the place apart that is green but tended by humanity. In the pastoral tradition, the garden has been a refuge from civilization, yet civilization seems rarely dismissed altogether. Hence, the garden has functioned in the traditional pastoral mix as a reassuring amalgam of the human and the natural. Recent criticism, however, has suggested an alternative way of defining the pastoral spectrum. Glen Love, for example, has suggested that "wild nature has replaced the traditional middle state of the garden and the rural landscape as the locus of stability and value, the seat of instruction" (203). If this is true, then a cursory examination of Taylor's fiction might imply that he has not expanded the pastoral equation to include wild nature. Yet—as we find with so much of Taylor's fiction—the depth of meaning reaches far beyond what immediately meets the eye. In fact, Taylor's frequent portrayal of troubled gardens suggests by extension that there must be some other "seat of instruction," for Taylor's gardens rarely offer the kind of ultimate refuge from civilization that represents a realistic alternative. Nat Ramsey's discussion of the old forest, on the other hand, overtly suggests wild nature as a "seat of instruction." It is significant that the "wilderness" of the old forest is not a completely secure realm. As a place of refuge, in fact, it has a distinctly threatening component in the way it represents the unknown and uncontrollable. A natural world represented as devoid of threat would be the idyllic and benign natural world of the conventional pastoral garden. In presenting a pastoral alternative that is truly wild, Taylor has indeed expanded the pastoral equation to include wild nature as a locus of "stability and value."

Taylor's mistrust of the conventional pastoral garden is vividly displayed in the recently published *The Oracle at Stoneleigh Court*. The narrator of the title story embraces his future spouse, Ruthie Ann Sedwick, for the first time in her basement, surrounded by tomato plants hung "upside down from her basement ceiling [so] the fruit would continue to ripen without rotting" (75). Ruthie Ann is the narrator's salvation in an awkward personal crisis resulting from the volatile mix of a previous love affair, a matchmaking aunt, and his own feelings of self-doubt and inadequacy. And by the end of the story, he and Ruthie Ann have settled into her house with her mother where they garden, read, and enjoy the "uneventful seclusion" (88) that seems to make their lives full. Yet we don't share the narrator's contentment. The "peace" he finds in being free from "wandering thoughts" (88) about former friends strikes us as smug and overly complacent. His retreat to Ruthie Ann Sedwick's tomatoes is more an escape to a hermetic and illusory garden of denial than an ascent to a true pastoral place of "stability and value." Their garden of ever-ripening tomatoes is the garden of the conventional pastoral ideal, and Taylor seems to be saying that such an Edenic site has no place in modern fiction as a "seat of instruction," unless of course it instructs by negative example.

It is in the form of negative example that Taylor's pastoral vision seems to define itself and operate with the most consistency. More often than not, Taylor seems to be suggesting that simplistic idealization of nature—that is, defining it in the purely human terms of the pastoral garden—is as problematic for society as is complete rejection of it in favor of urban civilization. It is rare that wild nature is overtly posited as the preferable alternative in the pastoral equation, as it is in "The Old Forest," but the persistent failure of the idealized garden—as well as urban civilization—in the bulk of Taylor's narratives suggests wild nature perforce. But this is not to imply that Taylor's pastoral equation itself is constant. Taylor seems to want to play off the moving target of the American pastoral mode in as many ways as he can. And it is precisely because he exhibits no compulsion to ossify his approach to the motifs of pastoral writing that he has been and continues to be a fascinating writer.

Peter Taylor and the Negotiation of Absence

CHRISTOPHER P. METRESS

In a 1985 interview with Hubert H. McAlexander, Peter Taylor reflected on the many houses he has owned and restored. After briefly mentioning that he and his wife had once owned Faulkner's old residence in Charlottesville, Taylor reached back into his family past in order to explain his fascination with houses, offering us the following history:

> The Taylors were all great builders, and my own family moved around a great deal and lived in a number of houses. Two images stick in my mind from my own family's history. Just before my paternal grandfather died and my father decided to leave the little town of Trenton and go to Nashville, my father had chosen a site for a house just outside Trenton. When we went back there later on visits, we'd often go out to the site; trees had been cleared and some of the materials brought there. . . . The other image is from St. Louis. My father was president of an insurance company, and we lived in a huge, grand house on Washington Terrace, three stories and a basement. Then the depression came, and we had to leave that house. I went back years later to visit my sister who lived in St. Louis. The house had been torn down; even the basement was gone. There was just a great hole in the earth. Those two images are haunting—the life that was never to be and the life that could never be again. (qtd. in McAlexander, *Conversations* 121)

With these last words—"the life that was never to be and the life that could never be again"—Taylor offers us a persuasive and revealing interpretation of the two "haunting" images of his family history. Taylor's own reading, however, does not exhaust the significance of these two resonant images, for the cleared field in Trenton and the "great hole" in St. Louis contain more than just this message of histories unconsummated and histories erased. Rather, a more rewarding interpretation of these two images might focus on how each one dramatizes the significance of absence in the generation and construction of meaning. For instance, each image in and of itself carries little significance. Were we to drive past the cleared field in Trenton, we would see little more than a cleared field. Were we to drive down Washington Terrace in St. Louis, we would see little more than a great hole in the earth. What is "present" in each image, what is "there," reveals little. However, what is "absent" from each image, what is "*not* there," reveals everything and fills that which is present with greater significance. The house that was never built, the great house that was torn down—we must know of these absences if we are ever to know the meaning of the presences that lie before us. Without knowledge of these absences, our interpretative capabilities, the means by which we generate and construct meaning, are seriously limited, perhaps even deeply flawed. In order to apprehend the significance of these two images, we must know the absences that inform them.

The knowledge of absence that is central to these two images is also central to any understanding of Peter Taylor's fiction. This holds true because we can say of Taylor's fiction what Tsvetan Todorov has said of Henry James's short stories—that is, on reading the master's work we discover, "The essential is absent, the absence is essential" (145). Therefore, to encounter Taylor's images of the cleared field and the great hole and to read them with eye for both absence and presence not only permits us to appreciate more fully their haunting vitality for Peter Taylor, but it also allows us to understand more completely how to read a Peter Taylor story: we must seek out the absences because the absences are essential.

For instance, Taylor's 1963 story "Two Pilgrims" demands an encounter with absence similar to the one generated by Taylor's comments to McAlexander. The narrator of the story recalls a car trip he took when he was seventeen years old. Serving as a chauffeur to his uncle and Mr. Lowder, the uncle's client in a pending lawsuit, the narrator must drive from Memphis to northern Alabama. During the trip, the narrator recalls, the two older men "talked of almost nothing but bird dogs and field trials, interrupting themselves only when we passed through some little town or settlement to speak of the fine people they knew who had once lived there" (*CS* 216). Most of the trip contains such talk, whether it be references to the rounding up of the Cherokees by Winfield Scott in 1838 near Waynesboro or the three-hour breakfast enjoyed by the uncle in a house with a neoclassic portico in La Grange.

The trip is disrupted, however, as the men enter the Natchez Trace section just south of Waynesboro. Coming upon a modest country house set afire, the narrator slows down, and the uncle and Mr. Lowder jump from the car, promising the woman of the house that they will save whatever they can. Soon they are "hurling bedclothes and homemade-looking stools and chairs through the side windows . . . [and] dashing out across the porch and into the yard, deposit[ing] on the ground a big pitcher and washbasin or a blurry old mirror with a carved wooden frame" (220).

After this almost comic rescue of worthless objects, Mr. Lowder picks up an infant's chamber pot and asks the woman the whereabouts of her child. Her response confirms the worst, and the narrator and his uncle rush back into the blazing house but are unable to find the child. Just as they leap off the back stoop of the house, "the rafters and the whole roof above the kitchen came down" (224). Moments later, the woman's husband comes out of the barn behind the house and holds in his hands the sought-after child. When the husband finds out that his wife told the men that their child was still in the house, he strikes her. When the men seek to defend the woman, the husband tells them, "She knowed this here young'un warn't in no house!" (226).

As the fire brigade arrives and the crowds gather, the narrator wonders whether his uncle or Mr. Lowder will tell someone of the woman's curious behavior. Neither man, however, raises the issue. Rather, the three men get back into their car and continue their trip. As they leave the Natchez Trace and move into "the rich and beautiful section to the east of it" (229), the narrator tells his two older companions, "Seems good to have finally got out of that godforsaken-looking stretch back there" (229). The two gentlemen object to the narrator's characterization of the land, the uncle claiming, "Every countryside has its own kind of beauty. It's up to you to learn to see it, that's all" (229). Mr. Lowder concurs, asserting that "if you don't see it, it's just your loss. Because it's *there*" (229, Taylor's emphasis).

We soon discover, however, that Mr. Lowder's concept of what is *"there"* is informed by a recognition of what is *not* there. The uncle chastises his nephew for not appreciating presences, for "How could you judge [the country]," the uncle asks, "flying along on a highway at fifty miles an hour, flapping that damned wiper off and on?" (230). Agreeing with the uncle that the young man has misread the landscape, Mr. Lowder adds: "More than that . . . you would have to have seen that country thirty years ago to understand why it looks the way it does now. That was when they cut out the last of the old timber. I've heard it said that when the first white men came through that section it had the prettiest stand of timber on the continent!" (230). The narrator responds to this call to appreciate absence by blurting out, "But what's that got to do with it?" (230).

In Taylor's fiction, however, this appreciation of absence has everything to do with encountering the full resonance of experience, and it is this very resonance of absence that the narrator must learn. At the end of "Two Pilgrims," then, after the three men have reached their Alabama destination, the narrator closes his story as follows:

> After dinner that night, [my uncle and Mr. Lowder] sat in the lobby and talked to other men who were staying there in the hotel. I found myself a place near the stove and sat there with my feet on the fender, sometimes dozing off. But even when I was half asleep I was still listening to see whether, in their talk, either Mr. Lowder or my uncle would make any reference to our adventure that morning. Neither did. Instead, as the evening wore on and they got separated and were sitting with two different groups of men, I heard them both repeating the very stories they had told in the car before we crossed the Tennessee River—stories about bird hunting and field trials and about my uncle's three-hour breakfast in the old house with the neoclassic portico. (230–31)

Earlier in the day, the narrator had doubted the value of understanding what is not there, had questioned the need for perceiving anything beyond presence. For him, the Alabama country south of Memphis is godforsaken and nothing more. He has no knowledge of the "country thirty years ago," and thus he cannot see, nor does he care to see, the last stand of timber that is no longer there. At the end of the day, however, he is seeking what is not there as he listens for that which is not spoken. Where others hear only the stories told, the narrator hears the story not told, appreciating absences where others know only presences. Furthermore, the ending of this narrative also allows Taylor to create for his reader an encounter that mirrors his own encounter with the two haunting images of his family history, for just as Taylor perceived a cleared field and a great hole and then negotiated meaning from them by appreciating the absences that informed each image, so too must Taylor's readers now perceive the untold story informing the conclusion of "Two Pilgrims" and then negotiate the meaning generated by a knowledge of such absence. No reading of this story can be fully achieved without somehow accounting for what is not said "[a]fter dinner that night." Here then, at the end of "Two Pilgrims," we have a moment that bears testament to James Curry Robison's assertion that Taylor's fiction is concerned "with powerful expectations, with manners, with crucial things unsaid. Frequently in his scenes, the unspoken words are the most important ones" (12). Be it an "unsaid" story or a last stand of timber, what is not there is a "crucial thing": absence enriches presence, Taylor tells us, but only if one appreciates—that is, gives value to—that absence.

So much of Taylor's fiction seeks to confirm this enriching essentiality of absence, seeks to reanimate our encounters with the unseen, the unspoken, the apparently "unpresent" but always demanding portions of experience. Nowhere is this more readily apparent than in *Presences* (1973), a volume of seven one-act plays. In six of the seven plays, the "presence" is either a ghost or a series of ghosts. These "presences," of course, are actually "absences," for the ghosts are the unseen but ultimately vital forces that drive Taylor's characters to choose their lives of quiet and genteel desperation. (One is reminded, once again, of Todorov on James: "Henry James always speaks of ghosts as *presences*. . . . [For James] the essence [of life] is never present except if it is a ghost, that is, absence par excellence" [154–55].) The first play in the volume, "Two Images," is representative of Taylor's intent. Meg, a thirty-five-year-old woman married four times over, and Nicky, her younger brother, meet one afternoon in Meg's house. Nicky is set on extracting money from his wealthy sister, who is equally intent on resisting his pleas and reminding him how he squandered their beloved father's fortune. In the course of their contentious discussion, each sibling summons up a competing apparition of their dead father. Nicky's memory of his father as sexually promiscuous and hypocritically judgmental leads him to summon up an apparition who appears timid and uncertain. Nicky is thus able to dominate this presence and through it to berate his father as his father once berated him. Meg's apparition is of a different order. Her father comes to her as a fastidiously dressed gentleman because she, unlike Nicky, has idealized her father. Nicky's apparition, we learn, has appeared to him many times before, but this is the first time that Meg has summoned up this presence. At the end of the act, Meg's gentlemanly apparition makes seductive overtures toward her, and she, without resistance, surrenders to his embrace. As Albert Griffith notes, "The point the play makes somewhat too explicitly is that Meg's erotic attachment to her father had always been a presence (throughout all four loveless marriages) but could not be faced for what it was until her idealized image of the father was transformed and released by Nicky's iconoclastic countervision" (rev. ed. 110–11). Another point the play makes, once again perhaps somewhat too explicitly, is that every relationship, every life, is haunted by some unseen but powerful influence. The ghost of the father, the "absence par excellence," not only stands between Nicky and Meg but also shapes the manner in which both Nicky and Meg negotiate an understanding of themselves and each other.

The men and women of *Presences* are forced to confront on the most explicit level what almost all of Peter Taylor's characters must face on a more subtle level—absence is essential, and our lives are determined by how well we negotiate this discovery, how well we recognize and come to terms with the potency of this absence. Absence, and the attendant negotiation it demands, is almost everywhere in Taylor's fiction, and, furthermore, it comes to us in a variety of guises, most of which are less explicit and more artful than the ghostly guises employed in *Presences*. For instance, several times Taylor has created suggestive titles that demand that we confront absence even before we begin to engage his narratives. In both "A Spinster's Tale" (1940) and *The Widows of Thornton* (1954), the key word of each title—"spinster" and "widow"—focuses less on what a person is—a woman—than on what a person is not—never or no longer married to a man. Both "spinster" and "widow" are terms that designate through absence, that direct our attention to what is missing from a person as a means of constructing a definition of that person. Moreover, the title of Taylor's third volume of stories, *Happy Families Are All Alike* (1959), also operates on a similar focusing of attention. Although the title of this volume does not contain a single key word that designates through absence—such as "widow" or "spinster"—the entire title itself—"Happy families are all alike"—cleverly demands that we engage the unscripted portion of Taylor's allusion to the opening line of Tolstoy's *Anna Karenina*: "All happy families are alike; each unhappy family is unhappy in its own way." To encounter the title of Taylor's third collection and not be engaged by what remains absent from the title—"each unhappy family is unhappy in its own way"—is to fail to perceive that which is most essential in the title. Once again, what is *not* present is as important as what *is* present. To grasp only what is scripted is akin to seeing only the cleared field in Trenton and not the house that was never built. It is only when we engage the unscripted words that we can fully understand the vitality that haunts and informs the scripted.

In fact, this type of engagement with absence is at the very heart of *The Widows of Thornton*. In "Their Losses" (1950), the opening narrative of this 1954 story cycle, Miss Patty Bean, Miss Ellen Watkins, and Mrs. Cornelia Werner must not only confront the recent or impending deaths of loved ones, but they must also seek to negotiate their obligations to the dead, must determine whether, like Cornelia, "We don't mourn people we don't love," or whether, like Miss Patty, we believe "Mourning is an obligation" (*WT* 16). Like the uncle and Mr. Lowder in "Two Pilgrims," these three women view the landscape and see both what is there and what is not there: " 'It *is* bleak,' Miss Patty said. 'See how it's washed. This land along here didn't use to look like that.' The two others nodded agreement, each remembering how it had used to look. 'This used to be fine land,' she continued, 'but it seems to me that all West Tennessee is washing away' " (13, Taylor's emphasis). Toward the end of the story, Miss Patty reasserts her sense of obligation to the dead, and in doing so she reveals her commitment to a culture that, like the landscape around her, has been vanishing into absence for years: " 'My people happened to be very much *of* the world . . . ,' said Miss Patty. 'Not of *this* world but of *a* world that we have seen disappear. In mourning my family, I mourn that world's disappearance' " (20–21, Taylor's emphasis).

The negotiation facing Miss Patty and the others in "Their Losses"—how to respond to the demands of absence—must be confronted by nearly every character in *The Widows of Thornton*. In a quotation printed on the flyleaf of the volume, Taylor reveals his own intentions in creating the story cycle, intentions that in turn reveal how his characters must by necessity see the world with a sort of double vision, must view the modern city in terms of not only what it contains but also, by comparison to the map they carry about in their heads, what it does not contain. "My idea . . . was to write a group of stories dealing with the histories of four or five families from a country town . . . who had migrated, during a period of twenty-five years, to various cities of the South and the Midwest. . . . I wanted to present these families—both Negro and white—living a modern urban life while continuing to be aware of their old identities and relationships. I wanted to give the reader the impression that every character carried in his head a map of that simple country town while going about his life in the complex city."

In his seminal 1962 essay on Taylor's early fiction, Ashley Brown observes that Taylor's characters "live a kind of double existence; their memories of 'the old times' (a very recurrent phrase) keep them from being altogether committed to the world around them" (596–97). In his dust jacket revelation that he "wanted to give the reader the impression that every character carried in his head a map of that simple country town while going about his life in the complex city," Taylor indeed wanted to emphasize the "double existence" of his characters. But rather than see this double existence as keeping his characters "from being altogether committed to the world around them," we need to see in this existence an arguably more profound kind of commitment to the world, one that is a "double existence" in that experience always contains two maps—the map of the present world and the map of the past one carries in one's head. The double existence Peter Taylor is after in *The Widows of Thornton* is an existence where one not only knows where one is, but one also knows where one is not.

Furthermore, in "What You Hear from 'Em?" (1951), also part of *The Widows of Thornton* collection, Taylor offers us the first example of a specific and recurring form of absence in his fiction. In "What You Hear from 'Em?" "Miss Leonora When Last Seen" (1960), "The Old Forest" (1979), and "Cousin Aubrey" (1990), Taylor introduces what we might call a "figure of absence," a character (or set of characters) whose absence or removal from the community generates not only anxiety but also narrative itself. In these stories, Taylor's protagonists must somehow negotiate these figures of absence and the powerful demands that they make, via their absence, on both the community and the self. Once again, these figures of absence heighten our awareness of the double existence of Taylor's characters because the protagonists in these stories are forced to think of their lives as being touched not only by those in the community but also by those absent from the community.

The opening paragraph of "Cousin Aubrey" may serve to explain the impulse behind the figures and the negotiations in all these stories:

> In the Tennessee country of my forebears it was not uncommon for a man of good character suddenly to disappear. He might be a young man or a middle-aged man or even sometimes a very old man. Few questions were ever asked. Only rarely was it even speculated that perhaps he had an "ugly situation at home." It was always assumed, moreover, that such a man had gone away of his own volition and that he had good and sufficient reason for resettling himself elsewhere. Such disappearances were especially common in our earliest history, before Tennessee achieved statehood even, but they continued all through the nineteenth century and even into the twentieth. We were brought up on stories of such disappearances. I very early came to think of them as a significant part of our history. (*OSC* 167)

In "What You Hear from 'Em?" disappearances and absences do indeed make up a significant part of Aunt Munsie's history. Awaiting the permanent return of Thad and Will Tolliver from Nashville and Memphis, respectively, Aunt Munsie repeatedly queries into the state of their absence because she hopes what others hear from them is that they will be returning to Thornton for good. Aunt Munsie's optimistic anticipation encourages her to believe that "there were going to be better times yet when Mr. Thad and Mr. Will Tolliver came back" (CS 243–44). But no such erasure of absence occurs, and when Aunt Munsie discovers that Thad and Will have betrayed her, she literally renegotiates her position within the community. No longer does she haul her slop wagon down Main Street, inquiring as to the news of Thad and Will. Rather, she takes up a position on the town square, where "she would laugh and holler with the white folks the way they liked her to . . . and she even took to tying a bandanna about her head—took to talking old-nigger foolishness, too, about the Bell Witch, and claiming she remembered the day General N. B. Forrest rode into town and saved all the cotton from the Yankees at the depot" (250).

The narrator of "Miss Leonora When Last Seen" states at the beginning of his story that the very reason for his narrative is absence itself—the absence of Miss Leonora: "Here in Thomasville we are all concerned over the whereabouts of Miss Leonora Logan. She has been missing for two weeks, and though a half dozen postcards have been received from her, stating that she is in good health and that no anxiety should be felt for her safety, still the whole town can talk of nothing else. . . . Officially, she is away from home on a little trip. Unofficially, in the minds of the townspeople, she is a missing person, and because of events leading up to her departure none of us will rest easy until we know that the old lady is safe at home again" (CS 502).

The events leading up to Miss Leonora's disappearance have to do with the town council's vote to grant a writ of condemnation against Miss Leonora's family residence in order to make room for the town's new consolidated high school. We soon learn that what bothers the town and the narrator is how Miss Leonora, because of the very fact that she is "out there," is beyond control of the town and could potentially affect the ways in which others perceive them. "[S]he is making it look very bad for Thomasville," the narrator claims, "and we want Miss Leonora to come home" (503–4).

By the end of the story, it becomes apparent that Miss Leonora Logan is using her absence as a means of wielding power against the very community that has just sought to wield its power over her. Her family, most of whom have never lived in Thomasville, have always controlled the town from outside the town's border. Now Miss Leonora is doing the same because she seems to be "orbiting her native state of Tennessee" (503) in her 1942 Dodge convertible. In a strange twist of logic, her disappearance from Thomasville puts her at the very center of its attention, and her absence seems to make her most present to them. At the end of the tale, the narrator reveals how he and Thomasville have now turned their attentions to what is not in their community—Miss Leonora—and how this absence has locked them in postures of uncertainty and anticipation. They are, as it were, controlled by absence, uncomfortably aware that they are being defined by that which is no longer among them. In the end, her absence paralyzes them because Miss Leonora's postcards, the narrator tells us, say "nothing about when we can expect her to come home" (535).

Peter Taylor's most recent collection, *The Oracle at Stoneleigh Court* (1993), continues to reveal his ongoing fascination with how the absent remains essential to the full experience of life and the full comprehension of experience. In "Demons," the narrator muses on those "voices one heard as a child" (89), voices that were mysterious and inexplicable and that one day ceased to be heard. The narrator, now an older gentleman, tells us that he repeatedly finds himself "in conversation with someone who insists he never heard voices as a child," but he refuses to believe these people because "You will notice one thing about such people: it is not only the voices they don't remember, they remember almost nothing about their childhood" (90). Instead, the narrator embraces fully a Taylorian "double existence," embraces fully both the voices of the present (which continue to be heard) and the voices of the past (which ceased long ago but continue to inform the present). In effect, he has learned, where he believes others have failed, to negotiate both presence and absence, to accept both what is and what is no longer. Thus, the final lines of his narrative manifest a powerful sensibility attuned to both presence and absence. Furthermore, these final lines not only recall the kind of vision that Taylor was demonstrating in the interview with McAlexander cited at the beginning of this essay, but they also remind us of the kind of vision Taylor was calling for in the carefully crafted ending of "Two Pilgrims":

> Whenever I return to the scenes of my childhood and admire the pale beauty of the sycamore trees and the glossy leaves of the oaks—almost like magnolias, some of them—I understand how far, in my mind, I have had to withdraw from trees in order to learn to love them. I go for walks in the woods with my family sometimes on my visits back home, and often I cannot help remarking on the absence of any chestnut trees in the woods. My family find it very curious that I remember the chestnuts at all, and tell each other it is evidence of how much I have always loved nature. But that isn't so. It is something I have learned. It is something strange and wonderful that I have learned to do. (*OSC* 116)

For Taylor such a vision, to see both presence and absence, to be aware of both what is and what is not, is indeed strange and wonderful. This explains, perhaps, his decision to include in this most recent collection three ghost plays from *Presences,* plays that, as we saw earlier, investigate the manner in which we negotiate, or fail to negotiate, the absences that inform our sense of self and our sense of others. Furthermore, in two other stories in the collection, the titular "The Oracle at Stoneleigh Court" and "The Witch of Owl Mountain Springs: An Account of Her Remarkable Powers," Taylor seems determined to generate this strange and wonderful vision that sees both what is and what is not. Both stories involve narrators who admit to moments of amnesia, and because of this we are forced to read both stories as much for what they do not say as for what they do say. What is said by each narrator is certainly important and cannot be dismissed; however, it is only when we consider what is *not* said, what is *not present* in each narrative, that we can perceive most fully the significance of each story.

A paragraph from one of these stories, "The Witch of Owl Mountain Springs," can help to conclude our discussion. Early in the story, the narrator attempts to describe the world of Owl Mountain Springs in the 1930s. The narrator's account depends as much on absence as it does on presence, on knowing what something is *not* in order to understand more fully what it *is*.

> Perhaps a realistic presentation of the character of the place can best be stated negatively. No one imagined that Owl Mountain Springs itself was exactly a fashionable summer place, not even vaguely so—not in the eyes of the great world, at any rate. It was never thought of as any Blowing Rock or Asheville or White Sulphur Springs. It was never imagined to be a Rye or a Saratoga or a Cape Cod or a Nantucket. It would have seemed laughable to mention it in the same breath with Bar Harbor or Harbor Point. And yet it was quite as much respected for what it was *not* as for what it *was*. . . . I suppose those who vacationed there thought of themselves somehow or other as the special urban remnants of an old gentry out of another time, out of their remotely agrarian past. Surely it was the things they did not do that counted most with them. It was the things they did not have and did not want that mattered most. It was what they were *not* that made them *who* they were. (119–20, Taylor's emphasis)

Just as the summer inhabitants of Owl Mountain Springs must know what they are not in order to comprehend most fully who they are, so too must we consider how absence informs everything that Peter Taylor writes. Because Taylor writes of a time and a place that are vanishing or, for that matter, have already vanished, his fiction quite often explores the unseen, unappreciated, and forgotten traces of experience, the ways in which that which is not or that which is no longer continues to inform all that is. These revealing traces of absence come to us and to Taylor's characters in many different guises—the eloquent silence at the end of "Two Pilgrims," the ghostly apparitions haunting *Presences,* the "absent figure" of Miss Leonora orbiting her native Tennessee, the hidden histories at the heart of "The Oracle at Stoneleigh Court" and "The Witch of Owl Mountain Springs"—but whichever form these absences take, they are always present and they are always essential. Above all else, however, these absences demand negotiation, demand that we appreciate their essentiality so that we may encounter most fully the haunting complexity and enriching mystery of experience. To negotiate the world by way of this strange and wonderful vision, to see great houses where others see only great holes—in story after story Peter Taylor tells us that it is something we must learn to do.

Peter Taylor and
the Paternal Metaphor

LINDA RICHMOND

A STORY FOUND in both "Dean of Men" and *A Summons to Memphis* seems to embody Peter Taylor's lifelong concern with the process by which the human character becomes fixed through a complex encounter involving society, language, and psychology. This story of a father's betrayal at the hands of his trusted colleague in the world of law, politics, or education and its lifelong effects on his offspring suggests a Freudian analysis because Freud developed the idea that in the Oedipus complex the structural position of the father vis-à-vis the child-mother dyad is what forms the nodal point of sexual and social development. It seems that in Taylor's story of a father who is betrayed by his friend and trusted business associate, a son whose professional goals are derailed after he witnesses his father's plight, and sons and daughters whose sexuality is forever stunted by the father's response to this event, we are presented with a prototype of the power of the paternal figure to determine the identities of his children and the role these children subsequently assume in the fabric of their society. Taylor is known for his economic use of language, and so his repetitive retelling of this story suggests that he is not only relating a vivid example of the power of the paternal figure but also attempting to master a traumatic encounter with the figure. According to Freud, in repeating painful experiences through games and stories, we gain mastery over them.

In the short story "Dean of Men," the tale of this betrayal takes on the character of a familial, if not universal, myth because the narrator relates three stories of betrayal: his own, his father's, and his grandfather's. His grandfather had been persuaded by some young former protégés to give up his seat in the Senate and run for governor, only to be defrauded of both the governorship and the Senate seat by these same young men. Thereafter, he retired completely from public life "to the bosom of his family," a household of women and children. The narrator's father studies law but avoids politics and becomes instead the president of a large insurance company. The company's investments come under scrutiny, and his father's old friend and business partner, Mr. Lewis Barksdale, is the only one who can straighten out the company's affairs. The son, who is telling the story, goes with his parents to the station to meet Mr.

Barksdale. Barksdale never comes, and the father is forced to suffer embarrassing publicity; thereafter he too turns his attention away from work and toward the family. The narrator seems compelled to relate this repetitive tale in order to justify the choice he made years before to become a "Dean of Men" rather than a scholar after he is betrayed by his colleagues at the university, a choice that also involved the dissolution of his marriage to Jack's mother.

Another version of this story of betrayal appears in Taylor's novel *A Summons to Memphis,* which illustrates how George Carver's grown children prevent him from remarrying when he is in his eighties, just as he had prevented them from marrying in their youth. The tale of treachery appears in one of the book's final chapters, where the narrator attempts to reinterpret his father's life. In both versions, the one in "Dean of Men" and the one in the novel, the father and son make repeated trips to the train station to meet the friend and business associate of the father's who never comes, even though they are depending on him to dispel the recent accusations of wrongdoing in the business. In both versions, the lives of both the father and the son are permanently altered and permanently linked by the defection. In addition, once the final train fails to produce the "father's friend," the mother either becomes ill or loses her influence in the family. Taylor writes: "From the day we arrived in Memphis it seemed she never under any circumstances had any sense of what was fitting or any feeling of responsibility with regard to the role of a mother in an old-fashioned family like ours" (20). Moreover, Phillip Carver, the son and narrator in *A Summons to Memphis,* claims repeatedly and unequivocally that his father's unfortunate business experience in Nashville and the family's subsequent removal to Memphis when all four children were in their teens had permanent and devastating effects. As a youngster and as an adult, whenever he thought of either the move to Memphis or the fruitless trips to the train station, Carver concluded, "Father had ruined all our lives" (49).

Freud mentions many stories and examples involving trains in *The Psychopathology of Everyday Life.* There he shows that missed trains and other errors regarding trains usually reflect unconscious intentions. These examples reinforce the barely articulated thought in "Dean of Men" and *A Summons to Memphis* that the betrayed fathers need not have responded to their disillusionment in quite the extreme manner they did and that they were only using the failure of their business associate to arrive and exonerate them, the "missed train," as an excuse. In fact, in "Dean of Men" the narrator notes his father's cheerfulness at the train station, a mood that persists despite the fact that his business associate fails to appear. And in *A Summons to Memphis,* George Carver is quite ebullient, as long as all the children are in tow, on the trip to Memphis when he moves his family out of Nashville so that he will not have to confront Lewis Shackleford.

All of Freud's biographers emphasize a train trip he took as a young boy, a trip occasioned by his father's business troubles. His father's textile business was failing because the Northern Railway from Vienna bypassed their home in Frieberg and because Jews were being made the scapegoats of the general loss of prosperity in the town and thus were not being patronized. According to Ernest Jones, Freud "remembered the long ride in the horse-drawn vehicle and his first sight of a railway." He continues: "On the way to Leipsic the train passed through Breslau, where Freud saw gas jets for the first time; they made him think of souls burning in hell! From this journey also dated the beginning of a 'phobia' of traveling by train, from which he suffered a good deal for about a dozen years . . . before he was able to dispel it by analysis. It turned out to be connected with the fear of losing his home (and ultimately his mother's breast)" (14).

In his autobiography, Freud confirms Jones's additional comment that following this move he never regained the esteem he had previously had for his father. His story adds another dimension to that of Taylor's sons, who lose their homes, their mothers, and their newly awakened sexuality because of their fathers' actions. Phillip Carver grieves for a girl of his own age, thirteen, with whom he had begun a youthful relationship before the move to Memphis, and he claims that he never regained his confidence with women after that time. Thus, in *A Summons to Memphis,* it is clear that this move involves a symbolic castration; both the sons and the daughters have their initial loves and desires thwarted by their father. Also, the narrator of "Dean of Men" clearly believes his son to be effeminate though he does not see that his son's character has probably been shaped by his own reaction to betrayal just as his was by his father's response to a similar situation. When questioned about the autobiographical source of the story, Taylor acknowledged that his father had been betrayed by a man "he thought was a great friend" but denied that his father ever turned his anger against his children. Taylor claimed, "My father was most adoring of the brothers and sisters and wanted them to get married." As a postscript to the story, though, he added, "There's still more life to those people fighting it out in Memphis and Cleveland than there is in people going off and living in the book world of New York" (Robison 136). The latter is certainly a reference to his literary protagonist in the novel whom Taylor thus characterizes as a lesser man than his father.

Who is this powerful father? In his "Introduction to the Names-of-the-Father Seminar" and elsewhere, Jacques Lacan analyzes the way in which the function of the paternal metaphor Freud had described determines the development of the subject. In *Ecrits,* in his postscript to his essay "On the Possible Treatment of Psychosis," Lacan considers the role of the lack of the paternal figure, which he calls the "Name-of-the-Father," in triggering psychoses. He writes:

The ravaging effects of the paternal figure are to be observed with particular frequency in cases where the father really has the function of a legislator or, at least has the upper hand, whether in fact he is one of those fathers who made the laws or whether he poses as the pillar of the faith, as a paragon of integrity and devotion, as virtuous or as a virtuoso, by serving as a work of salvation, of whatever object or lack of object, of nation or of birth, of safeguard or salubrity, of legacy or legality, of the pure, the impure or of empire, all ideals that provide him with all too many opportunities of being in a posture of undeserving, inadequacy, even of fraud, and, in short, of excluding the Name-of-the-Father from its position in the signifier. (218–19)

In "Dean of Men," the narrator tells his son that all his male ancestors have been politicians; they were all pledged to uphold the law. George Carver in *A Summons to Memphis* is a lawyer. Phillip Carver in the novel and the narrator in "Dean of Men" are both children when their fathers are betrayed by the men for whom they work; both children are taken to the train station to meet and, by implication, appease the men who ultimately betray their fathers. In *A Summons to Memphis* Peter Taylor endows this betrayal with cosmic consequences. He writes:

> Though it is with present-day events in my family's life that I am primarily concerned here, still certain events of the past will have to be dredged up if present events are to be fully comprehended. For instance, it will be necessary to say something about my father's break with Mr. Lewis Shackleford, in Nashville, and to show something of that break's effect upon my two sisters, as well as upon the lives of my mother and my late brother, and ultimately even its effect upon my own life with Holly Kaplan. And I cannot resist this opportunity to point out how the evil which men like Lewis Shackleford do, men who have come to power either through the use of military force or through preaching the Word of God or through the manipulation of municipal bonds, as was Mr. Shackleford's case, how the evil they do, that is to say, has its effect finally not merely upon its immediate victims (in the moment of killing or deceiving or cheating) but also at last upon myriads of persons in all the millennia to come. . . . If all this seems an unnecessary digression in these notes I am making on my family's life, at least it will give some idea of the passion I can be brought to feel even today by my own mention of Lewis Shackleford's name. (15–16)

The passion and hyperbole of the above passage parallel the "ravaging effects" mentioned in the earlier quotation from Lacan, effects that result from any disturbance in the paternal metaphor, particularly in cases where the actual father is in a position of embodying ethical or societal values. Taylor also emphasizes the resonance of the name of the man who caused these effects. The fathers in Taylor's fiction control the use of this name; they prohibit anyone in their families from mentioning the name of the man who betrayed them. There is some suggestion that their sons could have escaped some of the debilitating effects of paternal power if they had chosen careers that gave them the power of language that their fathers monopolize. Alex Mercer in *A Summons to Memphis* tries to convince Phillip Carver to teach, but instead Phillip returns to his "serene" life with Holly Kaplan in the apartment in Manhattan, where he collects rare books. Here, he even imagines that he and Holly will someday just fade away because they will hardly have life enough in them to die. And the narrator in "Dean of Men" gives up his teaching career and concludes: "One sacrifices something. One sacrifices, for instance, the books one might have written after that first one. More important, one may sacrifice the love, even the acquaintance of one's children. One loses something of one's self even. But . . . [a] man must somehow go on living among men" (38).

Taylor, who says he had his finest battle with his father over whether he would agree to study law rather than pursue his literary ambitions (qtd. in Dean 30), did not just become a member of the "book world" like Phillip Carver in *A Summons to Memphis*. As a writer, Taylor is not locked into strict gender definitions, and he can manipulate the power of the paternal metaphor. He told Robert Daniel in 1983 that he was working on a long manuscript that

> takes place in Nashville and Memphis and Chattanooga. They are not the real cities of Memphis and Nashville and Chattanooga. They're mythical cities. I don't worry about whether I'm portraying them right; I have these cities that are useful to me, representing certain values and certain things. It's based largely on my father's life and my relationship to my father. I get involved in something like that, and for days I'll think about that. I think writing is discovery. You discover what you know about something or what you feel about things. For me it is this way. Instead of setting out with some social idea or scene or something, I discover what I think about something by writing. I've always done that. I've discovered all sorts of motives, for instance, in my father's life and in my own and in other people's. One of the great delights of it is not having to tell the literal truth. You wander off and imagine how you might have liked it to be. A lot of writing is wishful thinking. (42)

In an interview with James Curry Robison, Taylor was asked why he had switched from the feminine viewpoint, which he had used extensively in his early fiction, to a masculine viewpoint. Taylor's reply, an outgrowth of their discussion of "A Spinster's Tale," shows that he believes that for writers gender affiliations are neither rigid nor predetermined: "I was terribly aware that women had much more sensibility than men, generally, and it seemed a limiting factor in producing a story's point of view, domestic and all that. What it is for me—writing is always sort of playing around and exploring things, and I exhausted the energy, the impulse, to do that with women's points of view. I began to be more interested in my own life. I began to be more sympathetic with men after a certain point" (Robison 135).

Thus, Taylor explored alternative sexual personae, but his characters who are confronted by evidence of the threat of betrayal often seem to assume rigid sexual roles as a defense. Either they retreat into a partial denial or repression of their own sexual identity, like Elizabeth in "A Spinster's Tale," the grandfather and father of the narrator in "Dean of Men," and the narrator in *A Summons to Memphis,* or they embrace a stereotyped definition of their sexual identity, as in the case of "The Fancy Woman," "A Wife of Nashville," and the narrator of "Dean of Men." Many Taylor protagonists undergo an experience that imprints gender and societal loyalties on them, and these experiences are sometimes embodied in a single word or phrase. In "Reservations," for instance, the different circumstances of the bride's and groom's upbringing are summarized in the word "settled." In "The Other Times," the young protagonist has trouble reconciling the fact that the woman he admires is "well-bred" and "well-to-do" but capable of loving her uncle, who is a high school civics teacher. In "At the Drugstore," Matt Donelson's wife's project of "winning him back to his family" has meanings for him that she can hardly guess at. Often, Taylor's characters assume their identified role in society in the course of the story, as in the case of Elizabeth in "A Spinster's Tale," Josephine in "The Fancy Woman," and Helen Ruth in "A Wife of Nashville."

It is also apparent that, for Taylor, a subject's gender affiliation, in addition to all the other social loyalties, is determined by a confrontation with treachery and deceit. The narrators in "Dean of Men" and "A Spinster's Tale," for instance, seem to choose their gender characteristics, and they do so only when confronted with experiences in which they feel they have been betrayed. In "Dean of Men," the narrator prefaces his remarks by an introduction regarding gender roles that at first seems tangential to his main point but is really an integral part of the story. He says to his son: "I am not unsympathetic to your views on the state of the world in general. From the way you wear your hair and from the way you dress I do find it difficult to decide whether you or that young girl you say you are about to marry is going to play the male role in your marriage—or the female role. But even that I don't find offensive" (CS 3).

By the story's end, however, it is clear that he probably does find this confusion of sex roles offensive but that he hopes that in some way his tale of the ways in which he and his father and grandfather dealt with deceit and betrayal will enable Jack to assume the true masculine role. His response to the betrayal that he experienced was substantially different from that of his forbears. They retreated from the public arena into the world of women, and he accepted the help of one of the people who was implicated in the plot against him. Robison claims: "In this chronicle of betrayal, the ultimate Judas is the narrator, who betrays himself" (82). But the narrator of the story says: "A man must somehow go on living among men, Jack. A part of him must. It is important to broaden one's humanity, but it is important to remain a mere man, too"(CS

38). This statement does not allow for any accommodation between the two alternatives; the son is being told he must deny female power or be emasculated by it. In *A Summons to Memphis,* when, as old men, his father and Lewis Shackleford are effortlessly reconciled, Phillip Carver muses: "I could think only that indirectly at least it was this Lewis Shackleford who had affected my life so that I would become a man who would find it so difficult to fall in love with a woman that it could happen only once in my life. I felt my narrowness and cowardice about love was all due, inadvertently or otherwise, to my father's treatment of me and Lewis's treatment of my father" (192).

Thus Taylor's male narrators in *A Summons to Memphis* and "Dean of Men" assume their adult roles as men in society in response to their fathers and grandfathers. Their lives and choices seem predetermined by their male progenitors whose own lives are tightly bound by the symbolic order of custom and language into which they have been born. For example, when Phillip Carver attempts to understand his father, he imagines his father's birth and muses: "At any rate, the little baby George Carver was looked after by black mammies and maiden aunts, and when he was wheeled about the shady streets of Thornton, and led through the streets by the hand later on, he was looked upon as a little prince. Not only was his father the largest landowner in the county, his great-grandfather had settled there on a Revolutionary War grant, which somehow gave him the highest prerogative. Regardless of wealth or high station or education . . . regardless of all that, everyone in any community prefers a born hero to a made hero" (160–61). Moreover, when the family is transferred to Memphis, they learn to alter their dress and habits, although they never quite change their accents. In the case of George Carver, however, the way he dresses as he adapts to his new home and position is a striking aspect of his character that his son notes but cannot emulate.

The professions and loves of these sons are established through the power of the paternal metaphor in their lives. What remains elusive is the meaning of the bond between the fathers and their friends that is created and subsequently betrayed. Here the essay "Introduction to the Names-of-the-Father Seminar," which Lacan wrote in response to his betrayal at the hands of his colleagues and protégés and his ouster from the list of training analysts in 1963, may shed light. Lacan analyzes the Biblical story of the binding of Isaac at the moment when his own intellectual offspring were stripping him of power. He found in the story of Abraham, who bound his son Isaac as a sacrifice, the embodiment of all he had ever said regarding the paternal metaphor (*Television* 91). Lacan describes the God of Abraham, who demands and then rejects his sacrifice as "he who chooses, he who promises, who causes a certain covenant—which is transmissible in only one way, through the paternal *barachah* [blessing]—to pass through his name. He is also he who makes one wait, who makes a son be awaited for up to ninety years, who makes one wait for many another thing more" (92). According to Lacan, this covenant between Abraham and "El Shadday" creates a bond so that now "there we are with one son and then two fathers" (93).

Taylor takes great pains to establish the strength of the tie that initially bound together the two father figures he creates, George Carver and Lewis Shackleford. Phillip Carver describes at length the intimacy between his father and Shackleford, and in a quite vivid scene in the locker room of a swimming pool both men's families frequent, he lingers over his description of their physical nakedness, their ease in each other's presence, and Lewis's resemblance to a girl (187). Moreover, the Carver children, Phillip in particular, play an active role in this friendship. The Shacklefords do not have children of their own, and they warmly embrace the Carver children. In addition, because he is viewed by both as his father's natural successor, Phillip is often taken to the boardroom where these two men transact business. It is not surprising, then, that his parents take him to the train station to meet Lewis Shackleford, where his deception becomes a reality.

As Lacan explains the binding of Isaac (here Shackleford's name seems coincidentally appropriate), when the father "El Shadday" tells Abraham that he need not sacrifice his son, Abraham's reaction is to feel not only relieved but also betrayed. According to one Biblical commentary: "When Abraham learns from the angel that he is not there is order to immolate Isaac, Rashi [an 11th century rabbi] has him say: *'What then? If that is what is going on, have I come here for nothing? I am at least going to give him a slight wound to make him shed a little blood. Would you like that?'* " (*Television* 93). At this moment, in Lacan's reading of the story, a gap opens between the father's desire, and any possibility of fulfilling that desire. Thereafter, Abraham bequeaths to his descendants a belief in the special value of the gap between law and desire, which Lacan believes is symbolized by circumcision, and he prohibits his descendants from uttering God's name. After this encounter, Isaac's mother, Sarah, dies, and he, the son, is marked for life (94).

The fathers in Taylor's stories bring their favorite sons to the train station, hoping to appease their powerful friends, but the friends never arrive. After this event, the fathers refuse to allow their offspring to mention the names of these men, their wives become ill or are divorced, and their sons are permanently wounded. Lewis Shackleford/Barksdale make their friends wait and do not reappear until their absence no longer matters. Years later in *A Summons to Memphis,* when the son's character is already fixed, the former friends are reunited, but when Taylor's young boys leave the train station with their fathers, they have presumably come face to face with the gap between the strength of their fathers' desire and the difficulty of fulfilling it. To some extent, the loss of the father's friend is shown to be analogous to the loss of a woman: Lewis Shackleford reappears simultaneously with Phillip Carver's lost love, and the narrator in "Dean of Men" loses his wife. As men for whom the paternal metaphor has been fragmented, whose actual fathers' authority as representatives of the morality of their societies has been irrevocably undermined, the identity of these sons is determined by what they lack. They either choose a way of life that imitates the realm of women and become like the effeminate Jack in "Dean of Men," or they continue to seek to become the father, the dean, the lawgiver, like the narrator in "Dean of Men." The explanation for the recurrence of this story in Taylor's fiction can be found in the selection on the treatment of psychosis mentioned earlier. Lacan explains that the failure of the paternal metaphor interrupts "the signifying chain, as inaugurated by the primordial symbolization (made manifest in the game Fort! Da!, which Freud revealed as lying at the origin of the repetition compulsion)" (*Ecrits* 215). Lacan is referring to Freud's explanation for the games children play that seem to reenact the painful experience of separation: they repeatedly throw a toy away. He uses the same reasoning to explain the traumatic experiences about which adults dream and literary artists write painful stories. This then is the third alternative to trauma and betrayal, which Taylor's protagonists reject by not becoming writers but which is represented by Taylor's writing of this story over and over again. The writer can seek through language to recover what has been lost, the paternal metaphor embodying both law and desire, the two friends reunited.

Essays on Specific Works

"Some Kind of Sign"

The Psychological Dynamics of "The Other Times"

DAVID M. ROBINSON

For its penetrating psychological portraits, unfolded through a discerning depiction of Southern class distinctions and manners, "The Old Forest" is sure to gain increasing recognition as one of Peter Taylor's masterpieces. But original as that story is, Taylor's readers will recognize its kinship, on several levels, to a number of other stories that preceded it. Aside from being one of his best, "The Old Forest" may be Taylor's most "characteristic" story as well. One element of the kinship of "The Old Forest" with a previous story was underlined when Steven Ross, in making a film version of the story, drew on scenes from the speakeasy roadhouse depicted in "The Other Times," a 1957 *New Yorker* story that Taylor included in both *Happy Families Are All Alike* (1959) and his 1969 *Collected Stories.*[1] Aunt Martha's Tavern, the scene of most of the important actions in "The Other Times," is transposed in the film into The Cellar, the tavern operated, we finally discover, by Lee Ann Deehart's grandmother, Mrs. Power.

Ross was, of course, interested in the more detailed depictions of Aunt Martha's Tavern in "The Other Times" as a means of providing a richer visual atmosphere to the film version of "The Old Forest." But there are also important reasons why the similarity in settings should interest the reader as well because this superficial likeness indicates a deeper imaginative connection and may serve as a critical point of entry for "The Other Times." Both are stories that center on the maturing process of the narrator, although in "The Other Times" that process certainly seems to have failed. And in both stories, the quest for maturity is dependent on the characters' entering a marginal and uncontrolled social place, beyond the dominion of the upper-class worlds that have, directly or indirectly, formed their psyches. In "The Old Forest," that

---

[1] For information on Ross's use of "The Other Times" in the film version of "The Old Forest," see Taylor's interviews with Don Keck DuPree (1984) and J. William Broadway (1985) in *Conversations with Peter Taylor,* ed. Hubert H. McAlexander (Jackson: UP of Mississippi), pp. 55, 90–91. For general background on the making of the film, see Steven John Ross, " 'The Old Forest': Story into Film" *Sacred Heart University Review* 5 (Fall/Spring, 1984–85), 3–18.

"wild" and psychologically challenging territory is represented variously by the old forest, the homes of the Memphis working girls who are Lee Ann Deehart's friends, and The Cellar, the site of the family identity that Lee Ann has attempted to flee. In "The Other Times," that territory is represented exclusively by Aunt Martha's Tavern, where the narrator takes Letitia Ramsey after escaping a formal Memphis party.

"The Other Times" is thus an important early instance of Taylor's use of a motif that contrasts an artificial and insulated world, marked by the distinctions of social class, with a harsher "reality" that challenges that world and confronts the person whose psyche has been formed there. This motif of the dual world results thematically in a narrative of probation in both "The Old Forest" and "The Other Times," in which the narrator of each story undergoes a trial of character revolving around his ability to master the new reality that he faces or to come to some deeper understanding of himself and his more limited world.

Taylor offers us an important means of measuring the failure of the narrator in "The Other Times": his utter incomprehension of one of his high school girlfriends, Letitia Ramsey, who holds a high regard for her uncle Lou Ramsey, a teacher in Chatham. Ramsey is known to many of his students as "the Ram," a derisive nickname that seems to be connected with their class-based contempt for his commonness. The story in fact begins and ends with the narrator's uncomprehending and scornful meditations on the Ram and Letitia's regard for him. "Can anybody honestly like having a high-school civics teacher for an uncle?" he begins, (*CS* 81), but we balk at his assumption that we will instantly share his distaste for the Ram and other such "peculiar relatives" (83) with which many of his Chatham friends are afflicted. He mentions several such peculiar relatives and their relations with their families—Horst Hauser, whose relations spoke German; Maria Thomas, who "had a much older brother who was a moron—a real one"; and Nancy O'Connor, who was always apologizing for her old grandmother (83). These examples only serve to underline his narrowness and insensitivity, much of it the result of a suffocatingly parochial desire for conformity among his class of friends. In fact, the Ram emerges as the story's hero, a character with whom the narrator suffers by comparison.

The narrator partly realizes this, and his narrative can be read as a struggle between his desire to come to an honest, though painful, self-understanding and his strategies to evade the distressing truth about his faults of character. The final result is a kind of suspended indecision that prevents his complete self-confrontation, even though his narrative does contain lucid moments in which he seems on the verge of comprehending his failure. He remembers his nights of indecisive struggle during his college years, after the events of the story, when he wondered "how people would treat me when I showed that I couldn't make the grade and began to go to pieces." Those moments of deep insecurity are connected in his mind with Lou Ramsey, "whom I considered the most dismal failure of my acquaintance" but who was, nevertheless, treated with great respect and affection by Letitia. "This became a thing of such interest to me," he confesses, "that I was never afterward sure of my own innocence in the way matters developed the night of Nancy O'Connor's party" (86).

The narrator believes that Letitia Ramsey stands apart from most of his friends because of her curious regard for her uncle. "The point is that it was hard to think of Letitia's having this Lou Ramsey for an uncle," the narrator tells us. "And I used to watch her face when we were leaving her house on a Sunday afternoon to see if she would show anything. But not Letitia!" (82). The narrator's curiosity is a sign that he senses something both unusual and admirable in Letitia, qualities that include her family loyalty and her freedom from the shallow values of her peers. Letitia *is* someone different, and she represents to the narrator an opportunity to break out, in some small way, from his constricting views of the world.

The narrator seems to be on the verge of recognizing that opportunity, for he tells us about his constant and wondering observation of Letitia during the principal narrative sequence of the story. He and Letitia, along with two other couples, make a trip to Aunt Martha's Tavern, where they find Lou Ramsey and are saved from a police raid by his quick action and heroic self-sacrifice. The narrator's observations of Letitia during the evening provoke in him a confused and troubled kind of introspection, tied to his sense of insecurity in the alien environment and his larger need for mature self-confidence. This element of self-doubt is exacerbated by his uncomfortable self-comparisons with Lou Ramsey, a man who seems at home in all the situations that the narrator finds intimidating.

The narrator's derision of Ramsey is in fact a device to mask his own insecurity before him. As a civics teacher, Ramsey is a figure of some authority to the narrator, but it is more important that he is also an exemplar of masculinity, as his nickname "the Ram" might suggest. He is not only a civics teacher but also a baseball coach, well-known among the high school boys "as a hard drinker and general hell-raiser" (81). We first encounter him at his usual Sunday evening dinner with the Ramsey family, paternally playing baseball with Letitia's younger brothers—it is to the Ram that Letitia waves good-bye, daughter-like, when she leaves with the narrator on a date.

We are even shown that the narrator's decision to take Letitia to Aunt Martha's Tavern is in some respects connected to his complicated attitude of resentful admiration of the Ram: "The important thing to me is that when we decided to leave Nancy's wonderful party that night and take our dates with us out to a dine-and-dance joint called Aunt Martha's Tavern, something crossed my mind. And I am not sure that it wasn't something I hoped for instead of something I dreaded, as it should have been. It was that this Aunt Martha's Tavern was exactly where we were most likely to run into the Ram on a Saturday night, which this happened to be, with, of course, one of his girl friends and a couple of his athletes with their girl friends, too" (88–89). This is a remarkably candid admission that the narrator went to Aunt Martha's in part to display his own bravado before the man whom he had subconsciously come to regard as an exemplar of masculinity.

Whether Letitia half expects to see her uncle at Aunt Martha's is a harder question to answer, but it is fair to say that she expects something to happen there and that she is in the process of trying to determine what the narrator's intentions are and how far she can depend on him. For a girl of her social status, the trip is a form of adventuresome but dangerous slumming, and although she is eager to go, she also exhibits a strand of caution that the narrator notices but is unable to interpret. This is the basis for his continuing, puzzled observation of her, a process of observation central to the psychological dynamic of the narrative.

The narrator's first significant comment about his observation of Letitia occurs when she is waiting with him on the stoop in front of Aunt Martha's before they are allowed to come in. This is a moment of some tension because they all know that they are about to do something illegal, and the moment represents their passage from the world in which they have some control and protection into the different world that Aunt Martha's represents. "I just thought to myself I would steal a quick glance at her while she wasn't noticing," the narrator says, but when he does so he discovers that "*she* was already looking at *me*," and looking at him with an expression that he cannot at first interpret. "Then it came over me that there was something this girl was expecting me to say—or, at least, hoping I would say" (89). Letitia's expectation, as we come to realize, suggests that the whole excursion has developed into a test of the narrator's maturity, a fact that he is still coming to understand as he recounts the story some years later. Like "The Old Forest," the retrospective first-person narration of "The Other Times" dramatizes not only a particular sequence of events in the past but also the narrator's attempt, through their retelling, to understand them.

In this case, the narrator awkwardly brushes away Letitia's expectation that he will assume some responsibility and control over the situation. "I said the first thing that popped into my mind: 'They always make you wait like this' " (89). This is not, however, the end of this unspoken encounter between the two. After they go into the tavern, the narrator makes the uncomfortable discovery that the Ram is there, with two of his athletes and their girlfriends. As noted above, this was not, for the narrator, an entirely unplanned occurrence, and he makes another revealing admission as well: "But I have the feeling that when we walked into that place that night, I would have seen the Ram just as plainly even if he had not been there" (90). The test to which Letitia seems to be subjecting him, with her look of expectation, parallels his own sense that his trip to Aunt Martha's is closely bound up with his identity and his somewhat confused quest for maturity. In that quest, the Ram has become a figure that he subconsciously hopes to emulate, even as he professes a kind of scorn for him.

After settling in at the tavern and completing the ritual of buying bootleg whiskey from Aunt Martha's deaf husband, the narrator continues to sense a tension, realizing that the stakes involved in this visit are unusually high. As readers, we also feel this tension increase as the narrative develops and are unsure where the events might be leading. One of Taylor's most effective strategies in the story is his prolonged suspension of the reader's expectation as the events at Aunt Martha's continue. Will Letitia be shocked and disillusioned to find her uncle at Aunt Martha's? Will the Ram be resentful and perhaps aggressive toward the narrator for bringing Letitia there? Will some show of affection or anger break through the reserve of Letitia's relationship with the narrator?

"Ever since we got there, I had been watching her in a way that I felt guilty about," the narrator says, "because I knew it was more curiosity than sympathy. And I was certain now that she had been watching me, for some kind of sign. I couldn't have been more uncomfortable" (94). Letitia herself dimly suspects the narrator's confused motives—she is not in the least upset to find her uncle at the tavern—and is herself curious, we can surmise, about the narrator's reactions.

The ironic twist in the story is that its climactic moment—the police raid of Aunt Martha's Tavern—is less a test of the narrator than of the Ram, who proves himself more than capable of meeting it. His reaction, in learning about the raid, is to protect Letitia and her friends, even at the cost of allowing himself to be caught. When Aunt Martha tells him, "You better git yourself *out*side if you expect to git," he replies, "I don't expect to git," and then explains: "They'll have to have their quota of customers . . . or they might make a search" (98). By allowing himself to be caught, he ensures that Letitia and her friends can hide in the bathroom and avoid the police. This is, as we later discover, a fairly magnanimous act because the arrest costs him his job at the school. But his fatherly regard for Letitia and his selfless actions to protect her are impressive. The Ram's decisive action serves to underline the essentially passive, childlike nature of the narrator, who is herded helplessly into the bathroom to hide with the others while the Ram is arrested.

The impressiveness of his action is not lost on Letitia. The narrator observes, "I won't ever forget [her expression], though I certainly can't describe it" (99). Clearly the narrator envies this grateful admiration, but the story demonstrates how ill-prepared he is to do anything to warrant it. Insofar as the story is a chronicle of the narrator's being tested by the conditions of a very different world from his sheltered one, he resoundingly fails that test; the story that we read is in large part his painful half-admission of that failure years later, a compelling mixture of guilty confession, obtuse incomprehension, and wistful nostalgia to which he almost obsessively returns in memory.

The narrator does, by the end of the story, claim at least a degree of self-knowledge when he considers the look that Letitia gave her uncle during the raid. "Still, I do know certain things from that evening at Aunt Martha's Tavern," he tells us. "I know how Letitia looked at an uncle who never had—and never has yet—amounted to anything. And I know now that while I watched her looking at him, I was really wishing that I knew how to make a girl like her look at me that trusting way, instead of the way she had been looking at me earlier" (107). Even if we grant the narrator his recognition of his own desire for Letitia's admiration, his confession only underlines his continuing, unreasoning contempt for Lou Ramsey, who, we feel, has certainly "amounted to" more than the narrator has.

That the narrator continues to use superficial class distinctions to shield himself from a painful self-knowledge is emphasized as he continues: "It almost made me wish that I was one of the big, common fellows at Westside High who slipped off and got married to one of the public-school girls in their class and then told the teachers and the principal about it, like a big joke, after they'd got their diplomas on graduation night" (107). The narrator's envy of both the sexuality and the self-reliance of these "common fellows" is the same resentful envy that he feels for Lou Ramsey, an envy rooted in a deep and long-denied sense of inadequacy. That inadequacy is in part caused, and certainly nurtured, by his own sheltered, upper-class identity.

It will be plain by now that the narrator's problems are similar to those of Nat Ramsey in "The Old Forest," although in that story Taylor adds the potent symbol of the old forest itself and the complex psychological portraits of two women, Caroline Braxley and Lee Ann Deehart, to make what finally is a much richer tale. And while Nat Ramsey shares with the narrator a characteristic passivity, he seems to achieve a greater self-awareness and sensitivity to others and to progress during his story in a way that the narrator of "The Other Times" cannot. But there is one further element of "The Other Times" that deserves comment, a detail of characterization that might easily be overlooked when we focus on the narrator and his trial of maturity. While the three couples are hiding in the bathroom during the raid, they overhear the sheriff talking with Aunt Martha before he takes her husband to jail. He asks, innocently, how she is able to keep her children, who live with her in quarters above the bar, so quiet during all the noise and excitement of the raid. She tells him that, like their father, they are deaf. " 'Can't hear it thunder,' she said, and all at once she laughed. Then she let out a long moan, and the next thing she was crying" (102).

This extraordinary scene, which punctuates the rising tension generated by the description of the raid and Lou Ramsey's arrest, seems at first to be an inexplicable sort of misdirection of the energy of the narrative. But its deeper relevance becomes clear after we hear Aunt Martha's moving articulation of her reconciliation to her children's condition, a speech that is being overheard by the narrator and his upper-class friends while they hide trembling in the bathroom: "When somebody says they're sorry about it, I say no, it's a blessing. My kids ain't never going to hear the jukebox play all night, and no banging on doors, neither. It's a blessing, I say, all they won't hear, though it's a responsibility to me. But I won't be sitting up wondering where they are, the way you'll likely be doing with your young'uns, Sheriff. It's a blessing the good Lord sends to some people. It's wrong, but it's *something*. It's *something* I got which most people ain't. Till the day they die, they'll be just as true to me as the old man there" (102).

Although the story focuses on the narrator and his attempts to understand his failure to mature, this is its emotional center, partly, of course, because of the moving quality of Aunt Martha's vernacular wisdom. But she is not, we come to recognize, wholly unrelated to the narrator and his concerns because she shows by contrast how superficial they are. Her honest self-acceptance, her assumption of responsibility for others, and her powerful and all-absorbing love for her children and her husband make the narrator's vain and solipsistic struggles seem shallow indeed. Aunt Martha's confession is the story's moral litmus, which validates further the character of Lou Ramsey, with his own exhibition of honest and self-sacrificial loyalty. It lets us see more clearly the narrator's lack of these values. "It's *something* I got which most people ain't," she says, and although her "*something*" means primarily the afflictions of her family, it also means her love and commitment to them. The narrator observes this quality in the Ramseys and is unable to accept its value and validity. Letitia's expectant looks at him were, we might surmise, her attempts to measure his character, to see if she could find the qualities she admired in her uncle in the narrator as well.

Taylor's fiction presents us with a number of characters like the narrator, and they are usually the vehicles that he chooses to narrate his stories. When we consider some of the works in which a version of this character appears, usually as narrator— "Venus, Cupid, Folly and Time," "In the Miro District," "The Old Forest," and *A Summons to Memphis*—it is clear that this is one of the most distinctive and compelling aspects of his work. In formal terms, Taylor found a rich store of character complexity and thematic irony in such narration, and he used it to open the nuanced social world of the reluctantly modernizing Upper South. His urge to dramatize, Henry James's directive to all those who would excel in modern fiction, was satisfied by the interplay of past and present narration, memory and self-analysis, that this form yielded. Finally, though, he drew out from this strategy a moral perspective as well, centered on a valuation of self-knowledge and a recognition that moral failure begins in self-evasion. In "The Other Times," we find Taylor moving toward a full realization of the possibilities of this fictional mode.

The Thrust for Freedom in Peter Taylor's Stoems

RONALD J. NELSON

Having won the Pulitzer Prize in Literature for his novel, *A Summons to Memphis*, in 1986, Peter Taylor is probably more widely known now than at any other time in his long and distinguished career. Over the years, however, he seems to have been reluctant to write novels and, indeed, has published only one other long work, *A Woman of Means* (1950), a book that amounts to a novella. Instead, he has devoted himself primarily to writing shorter works — occasionally plays and poems, but most often short stories. His literary reputation, indeed, rests primarily on the excellence of his short stories.

Despite the critical acclaim his short stories have received, his efforts in a subgenre of the short story — which he refers to variously as "stoems" (Wilson [3]), "poem-like stories," and "broken-line prose" (Thompson 165, 160) — have for the most part gone unnoticed (see Kuehl). To move toward bridging that gap, I shall focus on how four stoems from his 1977 collection *In the Miro District* — "Her Need," "Three Heroines," "The Hand of Emmagene," and "The Instruction of a Mistress" — present characters who attempt to extricate themselves from the forces that restrict them. Several of the characters in these fictional works are, for one reason or another, trapped in masochistic patterns of behavior, yet are simultaneously striving to satisfy their innermost needs. Certain others of the characters — notably those in "Three Heroines" — possess an inner strength that enables them to overcome adversity. The interplay of these opposing impulses toward resolution gives these characters the tragic dimension that Arthur Miller describes in uplifting terms: "the thrust for freedom is the quality in tragedy which exalts" (qtd. in Weales 145). The fact that Taylor's characters' attempts to transcend the restrictive forces are often unsuccessful is, of course, secondary to the stature that the characters attain as they engage in what Miller calls "man's total compulsion to evaluate himself justly" (144). As Miller puts it, such people have an "inherent unwillingness to remain passive" in the face of challenges to dignity, to one's conception of "rightful status" (144). Despite their frequently abortive attempts, there is value in their endeavors because each character demonstrates integrity through an active determination to be in charge of her or his destiny, rather than its passive victim. As Stephen Crane mentions in a letter to John Northern Hilliard about his own quest for "personal honesty": "A man is sure to fail at it, but there is something in the failure" (qtd. in Stallman and Gilkes 110). What that "something" is we shall attempt to discover by examining Taylor's well-structured prose poems.

Taylor's stoems interweave elements from drama, poetry, and short fiction into narratives that disclose the essence of his characters' lives. He sometimes employs overt structural units to facilitate this purpose, as in the three divisions of "The Instruction of a Mistress." The other "story poems," as Robert Lowell called them (Thompson 160), proceed by a less overt, yet equally taut dramatic structure that makes maximum use of narrative tidbits of salient information in the present, with flashbacks placed judiciously to fill in necessary gaps or foreshadowings that subtly prepare the reader for the inevitable—all culminating in resolutions that ring true. As William Peden observes, "The drama of Peter Taylor's stories tends to be internal. It exists in and flows from the inner lives of his people. . . . Character, indeed, *is* the story" (154). Each of Taylor's story poems is a marvelously woven carpet, the overall pattern of which faithfully depicts the multiplicity of threads in the characters' lives. The prose-poems display such sophisticated workmanship that the reader suspects Taylor of deliberately following Poe's formula for the short story: "In the whole composition there should be no word written, of which the tendency, direct or indirect, is not to the one pre-established design" (review of Hawthorne's *Twice-Told Tales,* 1842). In fact, Taylor has said that "everything in a work must be functional, must contribute, must be working" (qtd. in Goodwin, "An Interview" 16). On more than one occasion Taylor has expressed his belief in the primacy of addressing this task; for example, "Character and emotional content should always be the strong elements [in writing]" (qtd. in Thompson 151) and "the poetry of character and context . . . is what I care most about" (qtd. in Thompson 162). For him, "the business of discovery of the real identity of the images that present themselves is the most important thing about writing fiction. Ultimately it is the discovery of what life is all about" (qtd. in Richards x). In short, Taylor's creative process of gradual discovery as he writes becomes the reader's process of coming to know the characters intimately. For both writer and reader, then, immersion in the story becomes a "process of progressive clarification" (Middleman 5) of what it means to be a human being in all its complexity. By examining the clues that Taylor supplies, we can come to a fuller understanding of the forces at work within his characters: their needs, their frustrations, and their attempts to extricate themselves from what restricts them.

"Her Need"

The first of the stoems, "Her Need" (1976), was suggested to Taylor by an everyday scene: "I was walking early one morning in Charlottesville and saw a young woman, thirty-five or so, with her teen-age son beside her in her car, as she sped along through the residential streets, driving him somewhere. And I began to speculate upon what they were doing, where they were going. I went home and wrote the story that day" (qtd. in Thompson 144). What Taylor produced is an engaging seven-page stoem that gets at the heart of the life of an unnamed woman who works in a position of trust in a bank. Taylor employs eleven stanzas to accomplish the task of suggesting how and why she betrays that trust and, in the process, herself. Within each stanzaic unit, there are lines of varying length that often end at meaningful points, à la Lawrence Ferlinghetti or William Carlos Williams, although without the oddity of stepped lines. As with these other poets, Taylor often employs line length to advantage by ending at strategic points to encourage the reader to reflect, however momentarily, on the fecundity of the content.

A close examination of "Her Need" reveals Taylor's ability to disclose telling details of the protagonist's life, especially those aspects that contribute to her recognition of and frustration with the way things are in her life. For example, in just three words that constitute the first line of the stoem—"Her girlhood gone"—Taylor poignantly (and alliteratively) suggests the sense of loss this woman apparently feels at the departure of her youth. The second line, "Her husband in the suburbs with his second wife" (*MD* 133), records the departure from her life of the man whom the persona significantly does not refer to as her "ex-husband." Taylor thereby intimates the sting the protagonist undoubtedly feels at having been rejected for another woman. As if to emphasize her dissatisfaction, Taylor wastes no time in informing the reader that the woman speeds along "fifty miles an hour and more / Through the congested streets of the old part of town" (133). Her excessive speed in such an environment testifies to her frustration at not being in control of her age and marital status as well as to her willingness to indulge in potentially self-destructive behavior. She engages in that risky behavior diurnally as she drives her son every morning at six o'clock to his summer job. The extent of his gratitude for her providing reliable, free taxi service can be inferred from his remarking "coolly" to himself that her driving is all that is reckless in her life and from his posture, as he "loung[es] beside her in the front seat" (133). His "attitude" no doubt exacerbates the situation. She is aware of the danger of her driving, as is intimated by her "nervous glances / At all intersections" (133). But she continues to act in such a way as to threaten her own and her son's well-being. Her "horn-rimmed glasses required / By her license" (133) do double duty by suggesting a conservative way of seeing things at the same time she invites trouble should anything dart out into the street. Rather than freedom (license), she is trapping herself. Certainly, at the point the reader meets her, she has arrived at an intersection of her life that may at any time become an arena of destruction.

The protagonist construes the opportunities to free herself from her routine life, in the form of proffered promotions, as restrictions. The apparent falseness of the bank president, who wears "horn-rimmed spectacles like her own" (135), emerges in such mannerisms as his leaning toward her, taking off his glasses, shaking them at her, and wiping the lenses and his eyes ("Neither of which need wiping" [135]). Such habits are thinly disguised power moves that seem intended to keep her in her place, as are his condescending "my dear" (135), "see here" (134), and "young lady" (135). This latter phrase particularly nettles her, a point that comes out through her reflection: "She's *not* young. / Ask her son. Ask her former husband" (135). The bank president's strongest importuning, which takes the form of " 'We think you're a whizz!' " (135), only causes her to realize that such a comment was needed twenty years ago, when it might have meant something. No one who counted, like her father, ever gave her an inkling that she was a whizz. Consequently, this information is delivered too late—an essential ingredient of tragedy—and by the wrong person.

At the bank she has virtually lost her sense of self and has been reduced to looking asexual (suggested by the fourth line break here):

the way she's supposed to look
—Not too feminine,
Not too masculine.
Neither man nor woman
Could find cause to be jealous of her.
She looks perfect for her job.

   (136)

Her job ultimately, however, is meaningless to her; only driving her son to work is important to her—it is "what keeps her alive" (136). Such a focus of course is misdirected and can lead only to the eroding of whatever life force is within her.

Her daily driving, we are told, is done to help him keep his "perfect record" of not being late to his summer job. Yet, as the persona insightfully reminds the reader,

they're always a little late setting out.
Can it be there's something in her
That wants to make him late? What nonsense.

   (137)

Her denial is an indication, as James Curry Robison notes, that she "seethes with resentment" (71). Perhaps her forgetting the keys, or glasses, or cigarettes—like her speeding—is motivated by a semiconscious dislike of her son, who has an unpleasant attitude and has become a "little man now / And knows already what a whizz *he* is" (137). She seems both attracted to and repelled by the boy. Although she apparently cares for her son, her maso-chism and sadism emerge whenever she drops a burning match on the seat of the car and gets a hot ash on her skirt or his shirt: "The boy is forever brushing at her / Or at himself" (137), as if somehow to rid himself of her. They both know that next year he'll have his license and drive the car himself. Then he will have no use for her, and she presumably will have no reason for living.

This projected emptiness, I believe, is a major factor in her decision to alter the figures in the ledgers, as is her latent desire to demonstrate to the men in her life and to herself that she is a whizz (137). Having lit a cigarette, "[s]he brushes the ashes off the ledger / With a clean sweep" (138), echoing the son's brushing her ashes off himself. They both seem to want to start anew, phoe-nixes that will rise from the ashes to renewed life after whatever sparks there were between them have been extinguished. Although she believes she is "too sly" (138) for the others, there is little "whizzdom" (one might say) in her transposing of the figures, for she is likely to be caught and forced to serve out her time in jail.

Her attempts to transcend what she perceives as restricting her will, in all probability, precipitate her downfall. Her transposing of figures in the ledger is done with trembling hand—an indication of her awareness, like her earlier nervous glances at intersections, that she is doing something wrong. Yet she does so deliberately, conscious of the probable consequences. Her mind antici-pates the questions they will ask when they discover her embezzling:

> Why did the queer old creature do it?
> What need had she to do it?
> What need? What need?
>
> (138)

Such questions, of course, invite the occult mind. Surely, she is following an inner voice that compels her to attempt to set the records straight, to compen-sate for her disappointments in life. This proclivity is what constitutes her "thrust for freedom," abortive though it is likely to prove. In the end the reader is left uneasily reflecting on the waste of her life and on her sadly misdirected yet deliberate efforts to free herself. (Part of her motivation, of course, may be to embarrass the men in her life. If that is the case, her efforts are right on target.)

Finally, Taylor suggests that the real difficulty is her tendency to think about her situation excessively, for at one point he uses the words "think," "thinks," or "thought" eight times in eleven lines (136). Moreover, the closing words in the piece are "carefully, thoughtfully, / She begins her first transpos-ing" (139). She willingly takes the steps that will release herself from others' expectations, even at the expense of probable incarceration.

"Three Heroines"

The second of the stoems, "Three Heroines" (1975), immortalizes three women who, unlike the protagonist of "Her Need" whose behavior is largely self-defeating, have transcended or are transcending the forces intent on thwarting them. Despite the considerable obstacles they must overcome, the three heroines—the narrator's mother, his Great-Grandmother Haynes, and Willie Mae—possess a positive, almost indomitable, spirit that will not allow them to truckle to circumstance. The unnamed narrator, on the other hand, has in his younger days tried to find freedom through independence and rebellion, but by the end of the stoem he seems to have cast off few of the shackles of ignorance and incertitude, remaining for the most part in the darkness of immaturity and purposelessness.

At the outset the narrator's mother, the first of the three heroines, is close to death yet is

> Dressed to the nines, and she is eighty-six!
> A gold lamé gown,
> Savage pearls in her pierced earlobes!
> Diamonds blazing
> That her Grandmother Haynes wore
> A century ago!
> In Washington City!
> Before the War!
>
> (143)

The narrator discloses that "[t]he exclamations are all mine, not hers— / And silent" (143). He is dumbfounded by her outlandish attire, given her age and health, and asks himself, "Who does the woman think she is?" (143). Although he is largely out of touch with the essence of his mother's identity, she knows herself well. She is a strong woman whose attire perfectly reinforces her character: she is "dressed to the nines," thereby indicating her realization of the importance the impending soiree has for her. The gold lamé gown suggests that the fabric of her character is interlaced with the strength of valuable metal; the savage pearls connote an irrational power as well as a precious gem; the diamonds, the hardest material known to man, blaze, intimating the intensity of the life force within her—in wearing her grandmother's diamonds, she passes down family tradition. This woman is not restricted by what other people think of as rational—she follows her own laws. She will not be deterred from attending the Golden Wedding Reception "of a couple she hardly knew the names of," not even by her "medicine man," the doctor who cannot believe she is there "[w]ith what she had *inside* her" (149). The doctor has diagnosed the probable cancer within her but has failed to detect her inner strength, her resiliency. She does what she must, like all those who insist on freedom and self-determination over what others regard as conventional wisdom.

This woman is consistently described in terms that attest to her stature as a heroine, from her "almost too silvery-white mane" (144) to her miniature but swollen feet, which are "forcibly shod" (146) in the miniature gold slippers by Willie Mae. This latter event combines a suggestion of tragedy (Oedipus [Swellfoot] and Achilles [heel]) with comic relief (when the narrator's mother says, " 'This is one Cinderella who won't lose a slipper at the ball. / We'll have to take them off with the can opener' " [146]). It is clear that, although she does not have long to live, she will go out triumphantly. And although her son has been a disappointment to her—her Achilles' heel, one might say—she has risen above the situation, trying to solidify her relationship with him, first by contacting him and asking him to chaperon her for the grand evening and later by holding his hand in the backseat of the car on the way home, speaking of nothing but the heroism of her Grandmother Haynes, thereby trying to convey to him a sense of the values he has for the most part neglected. Her strength of character, which she inherited from her grandmother, and her sense of humor (a trait noticeably missing in the protagonist of "Her Need") enable her to rise above her circumstances and prepare for impending death in a dignified manner. She is a survivor ("So few of her very own sort are left" [144]) who will die gracefully.

At the soiree, " 'some old professor emeritus/From the University' " (148) pays the appropriate tribute to her, after she gets off one of her celebrated bon mots:

Dear lady, with your high-piled silver tresses
And your golden draperies, you are
Like a Greek goddess mingling tonight
Amongst the mere mortals of the Country Club.
    (148)

The second of the heroines is the narrator's Great-Grandmother Haynes, whose strength of character was severely tested during the Civil War. Her husband was on the Union side, and her twin brother was a Confederate senator. With divided loyalties, she "never surrendered / To either side," all the while looking after eleven children (two of whom died), coping with a berserk slave, running the farm, and putting on "a dance in the parlor at least once a month" (152). Although people said she was "vain and frivolous," she was also "capable and hardworking / And brave, too" (152). As the narrator's mother reminds her son and Willie Mae, Great-Grandmother Haynes was "[p]roud and witty till the end" (145). Her "thrust for freedom" and independence allowed her to live exalted despite trying circumstances.

The third heroine, Willie Mae, is a black maid who prepares the unnamed mother of the narrator for the evening with "her powerful brown hands" (143). With a clear sense of the importance of the occasion, she assists the mother in every possible way,

> Snapping the golden snaps
> As she stands behind her mistress, towering above her,
> Towering even in heel-less carpet slippers.
>
> (143)

Willie Mae knows her mission in life: less to be servant than to be companion and friend. At the end of the stoem, it is she who understands fully why the mother had to go to the soiree, whereas the son seems not fully to grasp the reason for his mother's attendance.

The narrator—whose life has been characterized by "rebellions and desertions and incompetencies" (154)—realizes that he has not been as much a son to her as have Franklin her driver and "the good doctor" (154). But as he escorts his mother home from her grand evening, he is drawn as close to his family tradition as he is ever likely to be. The connections between mother and great-grandmother "never seemed so real" (154). Although at age fifty-two he is more in touch with his roots than ever before, he is at the end of the stoem ill at ease and at a loss as to the full meaning of what has transpired. The prodigal has returned but remains largely in the dark.

"The Hand of Emmagene"

The third of the stoems, "The Hand of Emmagene" (1975), is, as James Curry Robison notes, characterized by a "remarkable emotional intensity, and reading it is emotionally exhausting" (68). It is a story about decorum that compellingly involves the reader in "profound moral concern" (66) over a hardworking, decent young lady. Far from being a conventional narration about manners, however, it is a gripping Gothic tale of repression. It revolves around a teenager whose religious upbringing has influenced her so greatly that she is almost totally repressed. What one would first expect to be concluded as someone's asking her hand in marriage becomes a cruel and senseless tribute to the dark forces gnawing away at her internally. Her high moral standard in a world of vacillation and convenience compels her to move inexorably toward destruction—a frail moth to the candle. Ultimately, her fidelity to her sense of justice makes her too good for this world.

Emmagene, whose name according to *The Oxford Dictionary of English Christian Names* (2nd edition) connotes wholeness and nobility, has an integrity about her in terms of her religious affiliation and her work habits. Unlike the unnamed narrator and his wife Nancy's habit of attending "the nearest church, whatever it was" (84) out of convenience, Emmagene "traveled thirteen miles each Sunday morning" to go to a church that seemed always to be changing its name or "seceding from one synod or joining another" over "some disputed point of scripture" (85). Her primitive fundamentalism no doubt imparted to her a resolute determination as much as an awareness of the wearying effects of internal conflict. Emmagene also has an admirable work ethic, evidenced by her cooking and cleaning before the others are up without being asked by the relatives with whom she lives in Nashville.

Emmagene's coming to live with Nancy and her husband may have been her major thrust for freedom, to be done with her former life in Hortonsburg. Her high sense of purpose, however, is undermined by her involvement—encouraged and pushed by her hosts—with the boys from Hortonsburg, especially George, who seek sexual favors. Attempting selflessly to satisfy their needs, rather than her own, she becomes nervous and filled with remorse. In the house she begins dropping the objects that she earlier had fondled. With almost incessant pressure in the form of phone calls with no one on the other end as well as steady tap-tap-tapping of her suitors' horns to exacerbate her anguish, her resistance weakens. Ultimately, she chops off her hand with the ax that she had earlier wielded with disarming accuracy on "an up-ended log or a balanced two-by-four" (83), doubtless in an effort to be true to the notion of retribution passed down to her through the tradition of her church. Although such an action can be regarded as masochistic and perhaps even sadistic, it is also an act of determination to hold true to a high standard of conduct and so is worthy of our regard. Such fidelity is in keeping with her name, although her name obviously can be read ironically as well. In any case, her life is incompatible with a corrupt world. She willingly sacrifices her life to be faithful to an ideal. In the end Taylor presents the reader with the lamentably tragic waste of a life that held considerable promise.

"The Instruction of a Mistress"

"The Instruction of a Mistress" (1974) was the first Taylor story-poem to be published. It has three distinct structural units: an entry in the instructor's journal, an old letter found posthumously among the mistress's possessions, and a second entry in his journal. Robison sees this work as different from everything else Taylor has written in that it is the only one in journal or letter form, it employs blatant dramatic irony rather than subtlety, it is the only Taylor story that uses homosexuality and lesbianism, and its two narrators are "repellent" (64). It is easy to accept Robison's judgment of the story as being "so cold and cynical that it can finally repel the reader" (64). However, it is a work of extraordinary poignancy when viewed from the stance of the characters' being caught in a web of illusions. Although the instructor and his mistress manipulate others—he to reinforce a lofty ego and she to discover the source of his poetic inspiration—it becomes increasingly clear through Taylor's magnificent, insinuating style how deeply they are trapped in an inescapable cycle, thereby evoking our compassion in their search for fulfillment rather than our revulsion.

From the first line in the stoem, "I taught her everything she knows" (39), the reader is led to detest the instructor and to pity the woman as victim. These impressions are maintained throughout the first part of the piece. The second structural unit, however, reverses the reader's reactions as Taylor discloses that, far from being the victim, the female student has connived with her lesbian lover, Maud, to dupe the instructor into letting her live with him and becoming her mentor. The master is fool; the embryonic student, master. Maud and the mistress's objective is to ascertain "the germ of his creativity" (46) and to write a book on the famous man. But the mistress gets caught up in her life with the instructor, wanting to be in the limelight with him and, more importantly, to take the place of whoever was the inspiration for his poems. Fulfillment for her must take this form, and she forcefully warns Maud not to write again and jeopardize her situation—"If you know what's good for you, my love" (46). Her commitment to achieving her goal is absolute, even if it entails drastic action. At all costs, she must be first in his affections.

The final section reveals that, indeed, she had an automobile accident that appears to have been a suicide. That event reminds the instructor of a teenage boy who committed suicide because of his own rejection of the boy's sexual advances. The instructor refers to the boy as "the heroine of my poems" (55), so disguising a potentially embarrassing situation. Yet it is clear that the instructor "loved him no less than he loved me" (54). The instructor has been consumed by the loss, which has largely undermined his life and which has driven him to engage in the repeated modus vivendi of providing "an education" for young, promising female students—in the process perhaps somehow to replace his first love. That unfortunate cycle continues at the end, where he has brought "a new girl" (55) to live with him. Even as he is caught in a cyclical process, he continues to strive to break the cycle.

In conclusion, Taylor's fictional creations in the story-poems do not necessarily involve us because of their admirable traits but because of their unwillingness to remain passive in the face of indignity. Even when their perceptions are distorted, they attempt to thwart the powerful forces that inhibit fulfillment. Their determined efforts to transcend such restrictions speak to the resiliency of the human spirit and the dedication to achieving a purpose, even at the possible cost of self-destruction.

Emmagene's Killing Cousins

LINDA KANDEL KUEHL

COMMENTING ON Peter Taylor's work, Andrew Lytle has said, "Betrayal involves almost all his stories, but they are never simple betrayals" (14). Nowhere is this observation more chillingly demonstrated than in "The Hand of Emmagene" in the *Miro District* collection. Though this poetic narrative contains elements of the Gothic so often associated with contemporary Southern fiction, they are not used gratuitously by Taylor, who, in his subtle examination of victimization, skillfully selects technical strategies designed both to mute the sensationalism and heighten the irony of the story's shocking climax.

To begin with, the narrative is divided into thirty-one stanzas of what Taylor calls "broken-line prose," a structure some critics believe makes the tale's inherent melodrama more palatable. Making the story a retrospective account, Taylor further minimizes the melodrama by eliminating the dramatic sense of immediacy attendant on so much potboiler fiction. However, the most important device used in the story to restrain its explosive subject matter and to increase its ironic dimensions is the genteel first-person point of view.

While superficially conforming to the characteristics of a typical Taylor spokesman, "a man of middle age, gentlemanly and courteous and patient, who means to confess something to us" (Oates 299), the protagonist of this story replaces confession with accusation. But despite the judgmental tone he assumes in his roles of guileless observer and faithful recorder, his own words implicate him in a heinous betrayal of a young country cousin named Emmagene. Ultimately, this treachery helps to trigger her bizarre suicide, a death made all the more shattering by the failure of those involved to acknowledge responsibility.

"The Hand of Emmagene" takes place in familiar Taylor territory, Nashville, Tennessee, where an upper-middle-class businessman, a native son proud of his city and disdainful of outsiders, expresses attitudes he assumes his implied listeners share. As in earlier Nashville stories, these listeners are never identified, but an acquaintance between the nameless speaker and his audience is strongly suggested by the narrator's conversational tone, the in medias res beginning, and the use of unexplained proper nouns, definite articles, and second-person asides.

The narrator, providing no exposition, immediately launches into the background of some unidentified "she" who, coming to Nashville to find work, had taken up residence in his home. The lengthy and defensive narrative that follows—filled with detailed observation and extravagant rationalization—sounds as if it were addressing specific questions put to the speaker by known interlocutors, perhaps friends and neighbors curious about the startling events we learn of only later. His account answers the following queries: Where did this strange girl called Emmagene come from? What was she like? How would you describe your relationship with her? And, finally, why did she kill herself in such a grotesque manner?

The narrator deals with these questions to the best of his limited ability; yet the monologue is a "fragmentary form in which the reader participates in the creation of meaning by tacitly supplying the other side of the dialogue" (Culler 368). While listening to his recitation about the pathetic young girl, we learn that the speaker is not just a passive recorder but, rather, an active participant in her fate, and we are soon convinced that the most "civilized" human beings in Taylor's work are often the most dangerous. Although accepted at face value by one critic as "good people" with "wholesome emotions" (Casey 215), the narrator and his wife, Nancy, through deeds that contradict words, make it clear that Emmagene had little chance of survival in a household that professed gentility but practiced inhumanity.

The speaker, introducing the girl to his audience in the brief opening stanza, alludes to her admirable qualities: she was hardworking, selfless, and mature,

> not just some giddy young country girl
> With her head full of nonsense
> About running around to Nashville night spots
> Or even about getting married.
>
> (MD 81)

However, the next stanza commences: "From the very beginning we had in mind / . . . That she ought to know some boys" (81). Despite the speaker's explanation that this concern was motivated by an altruistic interest in their cousin because she was "kin" living under the same roof, he fails to be persuasive. Instead, the reader detects through indirection and innuendo that something more than selflessness drove the couple to seek beaus for Emmagene. What is left unsaid is that the girl, who on her arrival expressed no interest in marriage, frightened them into believing she might linger on as their guest.

Emmagene's hosts, devoted to a concept of noblesse oblige, cannot admit that Southern hospitality has limits; but in their case, hospitality easily succumbs to snobbery. Calling on the collective "we" (appropriately so, since he and his wife turn out to be co-saboteurs of Emmagene's future), the narrator makes excuses for the couple's failure to take the girl to "the Club" or to have "people in to meet her" (81). Although reared in the same small town as they, a poor country cousin could not conceivably be admitted to her relatives' elite circle despite their eagerness to play matchmakers.

During the entire course of the narrative, the speaker is ever anxious to dissociate himself publicly from this rural relation, fearful that her final desperate act will somehow taint him and Nancy. Therefore, he continually contrasts the behavior, the beliefs, and the appearance of the girl with their own. The patronizing portrait that the Nashville man presents suggests that more than geography separates country cousin from city kin. He begins by demonstrating the differences in daily routine between the strange guest and her rational hosts, for Emmagene did not follow their normal pattern of sleeping and waking. The narrator says that "the oddest thing about her" was the girl's commitment to work, beginning her chores in the "pre-dawn hours" and ending her labors in moonlight. Not only does he consciously promote the "odd"-girl image through his detailed descriptions of her obsessive activities, but he also unconsciously reveals that from the start Emmagene was viewed by them as more than simply an eccentric.

Although at this point in the story the underlying causes for their cousin's compulsive behavior are not known, we assume that she had offered her domestic skills in return for a home. But whereas these talents would have been indispensable in another environment, they were considered superfluous in a house full of servants and were resented by her hosts. The younger female's unsolicited assumption of virtually all domestic activity breached an unspoken code of etiquette, and her fascination with her relatives' beautiful possessions made them wary.

Nancy might also have intuited what her husband hides from himself (but not from readers accustomed to Taylor's self-deceptive narrators): an inordinate interest in his wife's cousin. Though he offers Emmagene's plain appearance as one reason for not introducing her to the young men of Nashville, she certainly held an attraction for him. His selective remembrances include the "little repair jobs" she did on his shirts with her "creamy" white hands; and, significantly, he switches to the singular voice from the more prevalent plural when he describes a nocturnal surveillance: "More than once I saw her out there in the moonlight" (83).

Like Tolliver Campbell in "The Captain's Son" (the first story in the *Miro* collection), Emmagene made the other family members apprehensive because of the emotions she aroused. As Doris Grumbach observes, "Taylor likes to use as a vehicle of threat the visitor who comes to live in a large house" and "outstay[s his or her] . . . welcome." In this case, the welcome was further jeopardized by the peculiar happenings that commenced soon after Emmagene's arrival. The narrator mentions that the phone started ringing at odd hours; yet when he or his wife answered, the callers remained silent and hung up. In addition, cars began to cruise past the house but sped away when its proprietors appeared to be home. The couple suspected that the calls and cars were for the girl, but a combination of Southern manners and timidity made them reluctant to question her as they would a servant.

Emmagene, fiercely determined to prove she was their equal, emphatically insisted upon this equality by reminding Nancy and her husband that the three shared common roots. Preparing "country dishes" served up in the pantry on the cook's day off, she tried to make them believe they "were all back home in Hortonsburg" (85). But nostalgic Sunday sojourns could not raze the rigid social barriers constructed by the girl's pretentious cousins. Although Emmagene and his wife's family "had been kin," the narrator is eager to loosen these ties by pointing out that Nancy and their guest, despite what the latter believed, really came from "quite different sorts of people" (84). Previously citing dissimilarities in bearing and behavior, he now offers as proof a disdainful description of the girl's devout affiliation with a "hard-bitten fundamentalist sect" (84), too religious to be fashionable. And this church had helped shape a girl too puritanical to be fun, for Emmagene, much to her cousins' discomfort, eschews smoking, drinking, and cursing. Such differences in style were looked on as deficiencies in personality and breeding that adversely affect those living with her.

But as anxious as they were to divest themselves of their visitor, a shallow, class-conscious mentality still prevents them from introducing her to some "nice Nashville boy." So, left with few alternatives that would not damage their overtly hospitable image, the couple decided to encourage a romance between Emmagene and the mysterious caller they assumed "she was too timid to talk" with (86), finally working up enough courage to question the girl about the constantly ringing phone. She responded as though they "ought to have asked her long before" (87). Viewing herself as a member of the family and not some distant acquaintance, Emmagene had interpreted their past reticence as indifference, much to the surprise of the imperceptive narrator. Heartened to learn there were quite a few suitors vying for the girl's attention, her host proposed that Emmagene invite some to the house; his suggestion, however, was met "with something like rage" as she explained that all these young men were " 'a bad lot' " (87). He tried to pursue the topic further, but he was greeted with a deadly silence soon followed by a discourse filled "with evangelistic fervor" (88).

The narrator confesses that, following this episode, he finally must articulate the couple's chronic concern: "How long [was] Emmagene . . . going to stay [?]" (88). Feeling guilty at the time about silently withdrawing the welcome mat, he presently attempts to explain why the girl was so unlike their typical visitors, for whom the door was always open. Although her host maintains that he and Nancy were happy to fill their large, childless home with "really close kin" or childhood friends, Emmagene was neither. She merely represented an obligation, a debt to be paid because the girl's mother, a practical nurse, had looked after Nancy's mother when the old woman was dying: "It was that sort of thing. / And it was no more than that" (89). Always alert to public opinion, he insists that the invitation was just a simple act of charity expected from people of their social standing. Even so, this gesture, like others in the past, was inspired by more than altruism:

> But we could see from the first how much she loved
> Being here in this house and loved Nancy's nice things.
> That's what they all love, of course.
> That's what's so satisfying about having them here,
> Seeing how they appreciate living for a while
> In a house like ours. But I don't guess
> Any of them ever liked it better than Emmagene
> Or tried harder to please both Nancy and me
> And the servants, too.
>
> (89)

Like the other have-nots condescendingly alluded to in this self-indicting passage, Emmagene also "appreciate[d] . . . for a while" (89) her hosts' largess before returning home in a coffin. Although her cousins did not create the girl's psychological difficulties, the problems were certainly exacerbated by the couple's callousness and hypocrisy, which become more sinister as the narrator seizes every opportunity to emphasize Emmagene's instability.

He especially focuses on her hands when drawing attention to the girl's unusual behavior because she viewed them as having a will of their own. These appendages remain a perpetual source of fascination for the speaker, who, aware of the part they play in the future, features them in various episodes. A prurient interest is revealed by his diction as he describes Emmagene "caressing" household objects and wandering through the house in search of "things she loved to fondle" (89). During one such expedition, she accidentally dropped a vase held in "her strong right hand" (89). The narrator, re-creating the scene secondhand from information provided by his wife, speculates that the girl was startled by a noise outside, "a car going by, / Maybe one of those [Hortonsburg] boys" (89), who enjoyed hounding her daily as she struggled to seize a new life. The shattered vase, which symbolizes just how fragile a connection she had to this life, also reveals the girl's tenuous connection to reality, as registered in her response to the mishap. Already familiar with her evangelical devotion to the Scriptures, the reader is given a strong sense of foreboding, piqued by the story's title, when echoes of Matthew 5 are invoked:

Emmagene looked down at the pieces, literally wringing
   her hands
As if she would wring them off, like chickens' necks
   if she could.

. . . .

"I despise my hand for doing that," she wailed.
"I wish—I do wish I could punish it in some way."

   (89–90)

After this episode, Emmagene's relatives seemed more determined than ever to force her into the arms of one of "those boys," so she could "find a life of her own" (91). They began a ruthless campaign, reminiscent of the one conducted by Tolliver Campbell's in-laws and just as pernicious. Even the narrator confesses in retrospect that their behavior was excessive: "I don't know what got into us, Nancy and me. / . . . I'm not sure what got into us" (91). The overzealous matchmaking still puzzles him, but he inadvertently supplies enough information to explain its origin. Far more troubling to the couple than the girl's erratic behavior and household presence was the slow realization that she expected to become a permanent fixture in their Nashville world, an expectation that simply appalled them. To her supercilious cousins, Emmagene had committed hubris, forcing them to abandon their benevolent facade and all the lame excuses hitherto made for keeping her sequestered from their friends:

Emmagene had got ideas about herself. . . .
She not only liked our things. She liked our life.
She meant somehow to stay. And of course
It would never do.

   (90)

The narrator, to validate his chilling pronouncement and to express indirectly what social breeding forbids him from saying openly, hides behind a lengthy dialogue he claims to have overheard between Emmagene and his cook. When the girl confided her desire to meet some "boy / Who lives around here," the cook, according to our unreliable narrator, "indignantly" replied, "Don't git above your raisin', honey" (92).

Emmagene, however, was not easily discouraged by her cousins' delay in introducing her to Nashville society. Different from the other guests before her, who arrived, marveled, and departed, this orphaned girl clung tenaciously to her new family, unaware that they had decided the "house seemed crowded with her in it" (92). Not only did she continue frenetic domestic activity, but she also secured a permanent secretarial position in the office building of her cousin so that he felt obliged to give her a lift to and from work. The narrator, unwilling to recognize Emmagene's deep emotional dependence on him and his wife, maintains that it was just a "strange . . . coincidence," a stroke of bad luck, that the girl wound up as his commuting partner, a situation he eagerly conspired to terminate. And when he successfully managed to do so, he also helped to seal the girl's fate.

Those troublesome Hortonsburg boys, who had been mercilessly but futilely pursuing Emmagene, were working for the summer at her cousin's place of employment. One evening, as she and the narrator were about to depart, the garage attendant informed Emmagene that a mutual country acquaintance named George was waiting for her. At these words, her city kin sprang into action, as if by prearranged signal, denying the unsuspecting girl the opportunity to reject this invitation:

> "Why don't you ride with him, Emmagene?" I said.
> I said it rather urgently, I suppose.
> . . . And I pulled off down the ramp—
> With my tires screeching.
>
> (93)

Thus he left the girl behind, abandoning Emmagene and figuratively throwing her to the wolves he himself had had investigated. By his own admission, "[t]hey were . . . an untamed breed," information he conveniently rationalized: "But, still, I said to Nancy, 'Who's to tame 'em / If not someone like Emmagene?' " (91). The girl, however, had made it clear she wanted no part of such a "mean lot" (90), a position so emphatically expressed that the narrator gives us Emmagene's own impassioned words rather than detached indirect discourse:

> "They are not a good sort. . . .
> You wouldn't want them to set foot on your front steps.
> Much less your front porch or in your house."
>
> (87)
>
> "They're trash! . . . And not one of them
> That knows what a decent girl is like!"
>
> (92)

After so many explosive denunciations, there could be no doubt in the girl's mind that her relatives were now cognizant of the worthlessness of these boys. Therefore, Emmagene could only assume that she was also considered unfit to know the good people of Nashville when she was intentionally left stranded in the parking lot with the "trash."

The betrayed girl was late in coming home that evening, and Nancy reprimanded her husband for his thoughtless deed, but both compounded it soon after Emmagene's arrival. Obviously seeking an apology or an explanation for her cousin's desertion, the latecomer got, instead, a quite different response: "She looked at us questioningly, / First at Nancy's face, then at mine. . . . [S]he saw how pleased we were" (94); instead, the girl began dating the wild country boys she had previously fled from and ordered them to pick her up at the servants' entrance, where she obviously believed her relatives felt she belonged.

Emmagene had tried time and again to prove her worth, attending church and school regularly, obtaining a full-time job, working tirelessly in the couple's home, rejecting the advances of disreputable males, and displaying a sensitivity for the finer things in life. But all these efforts were futile; when she responded like some fatally driven creature to the horn-blowing parade of cars, the couple never once intervened:

> She would come to the living-room door
> And say to us she was going out for a little ride.
> When we answered with our smiling countenances
> She would linger a moment, as if to be sure
> About what she read in our eyes.
>
>   (94)

Emmagene's cousins were delighted by her new social life, oblivious to the toll it exacted. The narrator even comments, "It actually seemed as if she were still happier with us now / Than before," but immediately contradicts himself by adding, "yet something was different" (94). To begin with, her "hymn singing stopped," and, to their amazement, the once meticulous and dexterous guest became clumsy and distracted, the narrator ever careful to catalog the household damage for which she was responsible. The couple never connected these outward manifestations of Emmagene's inner turmoil with her altered lifestyle, though a glimmer of understanding appears in the following recollection:

> We noticed how nervous she was at the table,
> How she would drop her fork on her plate—
> As if she intended to smash the Haviland—
> Or spill something on a clean place mat.
> Her hands would tremble, and she would look at us
> As though she thought we were going to reprimand her,
> Or as if she hoped we would.
>
>   (95)

The emotionally disturbed girl had come to Nashville to escape the youths who, from her puritanical perspective, encouraged sinful behavior. Fanatical religious devotion, exhausting physical labor, and dreams of a sanguine future were weapons against erotic impulses and past humiliations. However, her own worst fears were confirmed when Nancy and her husband encouraged their country cousin to date men who didn't know " 'what a decent girl [was]' " (92). And, ironically, her fragile self-image was further compromised by Nancy, who had previously seemed more sensitive than her husband.

In the culminating stanzas of the narrator's defensive account, the simple purchase of a dress proved to be the coup de grace that ended Emmagene's life. Overhearing the young woman on the phone refusing an invitation George had extended because she lacked the proper outfit for the occasion, her hostess rushed out the next morning to remedy the situation. Although fully aware of the girl's straitlaced tastes, which included only sober attire, Nancy arrived home with "a sleeveless, backless evening gown" (96). This dress convinced the already guilt-ridden girl that she was viewed as a whore, and the reader is left to ponder the older woman's motives. To what lengths would she go to remove Emmagene from her domicile?

Emmagene at first refused the gift, telling Nancy that " 'George, and maybe some of the others, too' " (96) would consider the gown a sexual invitation. When her cousin naively inquired whether the boy had "misbehaved," she received an unforeseen response: " '[I]t's my hands he likes,' she said. / . . . 'It's what they all like if they can't have it any other way' " (96). Before her stunned listener could recover, Emmagene, "[a]s though she'd only been waiting for such questions . . . gave more / Than she had been asked for" (97). She told Nancy that the frequent phone calls received were all obscene, containing words her cousin " 'wouldn't have known the meaning [of]' " (97).

The evening after this intimate conversation, Emmagene unexpectedly donned the enticing dress and announced she was going out. Always conscious of the girl's appearance, the narrator observed that she looked "[a]s if she didn't have anything on under it" (97), openly confessing for the first time (though still hiding behind a third-person pronoun) that "[t]here was something about her . . . / That made one see the kind of beauty she had . . . " (97). Nancy, feeling some remorse, urged Emmagene not to leave the house when the familiar horn signaled the arrival of her escort. However, the appeal was too little, too late; the girl had finally given up "searching [the] . . . faces" (97) of the couple for a sign that she was worthy in their eyes of a respectable new life. Her defeat is registered in one of the last comments she made to her cousin after the latter guiltily told her to break off with George: " 'He's not the kind of fellow I'd have liked to like. / But I can't stop now. And after *you've* [emphasis added] gone and bought this dress" (98). Although earlier Nancy seemed oblivious to the couples' chronic disregard of the young woman's needs, even she sensed in this very dramatic scene that Emmagene had reached an emotional breaking point.

The grotesque event that immediately followed Emmagene's final encounter with her Nashville kin is reproduced for the reader in detached, reportorial fashion by a narrator whose only reaction to the girl's horrible death is pride in his own grace under pressure. A "scream" that "could be heard all over the house" (99), followed by the squealing of tires, led everyone to the kitchen where an ax on the floor and a trail of blood ending at a trash can presaged the gruesome discovery of Emmagene's severed hand. Since the target of the pitiful girl's self-hatred had always been her hands, she had literally followed the biblical injunction: "If your right hand causes you to sin, cut it off and throw it away" (Matt. 5:30). Yet even Emmagene's amputated appendage did not shock her cousin into abandoning the role of innocent bystander, cool and collected when confronted with unpleasantness (like the narrator of "The Instruction of a Mistress," another arrogant man implicated in the suicide of a young girl). He mentions boastfully that he, not his helpless retching houseman, had the fortitude to call the police from the very kitchen where the dismembered hand had been discarded. Unfortunately for Emmagene, in her family blood was not thicker than water.

The narrator continues in the concluding passage of the tale to present himself as the aloof observer of a situation that obviously violated his sense of decorum but did nothing to prick his conscience. It is no surprise that he offers not a single expression of remorse or sorrow for the passing of his cousin. Instead, he studiously avoids commenting on the girl's desperate act and compounds this omission by shifting the spotlight to Emmagene's boyfriend. The despicable man at first commends George for rushing the dying girl to the hospital and then cleverly transfers all guilt and responsibility to the "big country boy" (100) while ostensibly attempting to defend this convenient scapegoat.

There is no denying that Emmagene arrived in Nashville with serious psychological difficulties, and though her cousins did not wield the ax, they handed it to her through their patronizing, subversive, and selfish actions. Therefore, when the narrator tries to charge the Hortonsburg boy with Emmagene's death, insult is added to injury as he delivers a presumably generous explanation for George's misdeeds: "George wasn't to be blamed too much," for he "hadn't had many advantages" and "had come down to Nashville" where no "responsible relatives" were available to

> put restraints upon him
> Or to give him the kind of advice he needed.
> *That might have made all the difference.* [emphasis added]
>
> (101)

We realize, however, that a simple substitution of the girl's name for the boy's would transform this explanation into an unwitting condemnation of Nancy and himself, the urbane, genteel couple who ruthlessly slammed the door shut on a hapless country cousin.

As shocking as the events in "The Hand of Emmagene" are, what lingers with us is the narrator's myopic vision and deceptive voice. His self-deluded words are reminiscent of ones uttered by other family speakers in Taylor's cacophonous chorus—the mother of "A Walled Garden," the father in "A Promise of Rain," the grandson of "In the Miro District," the brother in "The Captain's Son"—whose "blind mouths" hang them as they sound the discordant notes of victimization and betrayal. It has been said that the author's "view of human nature is pessimistic, because he sees . . . imperfectibility" (Pinkerton 435), a condition dramatically demonstrated in the Emmagene story and in much of his other fiction where narrators weave tales of narcissism, ignorance, and cruelty. Therefore, in this morally ambiguous universe, it is not surprising that Emmagene's killing cousins deny their culpability, dismiss their victim as deranged, and erect self-protective barriers that shield them from the truth. But these barriers in Peter Taylor's richly textured fiction are designed to be scaled by readers who recognize that omission and indirection speak loudly only to those prepared to listen.

History, Gender, and the Family in *A Stand in the Mountains*

HUBERT H. McALEXANDER

No OTHER OF Peter Taylor's major works has suffered the critical neglect of his 1968 play *A Stand in the Mountains*. Brief discussions in Albert Griffith's Twayne study, in a 1977 *Shenandoah* essay by Ashley Brown, in Walter Sullivan's 1987 piece "The Last Agrarian," and in a couple of reviews of the 1986 edition of the play represent all the critical attention given the work to this point. Taylor's plays are of course the least studied of his works and probably the least valued—but still it is hard to see why this drama (one of the two full-length plays he has written), which appeared at the cusp of Taylor's career, should not have been acknowledged for both the power of its explorations and its important position in the Taylor canon.

One of Peter Taylor's most complex achievements, *A Stand in the Mountains* is also his most violent work. Drawing on central themes of his earlier fiction, here Taylor dramatizes conflicts rising from the displacements effected by time, the choice of role offered by a changing social order, the struggle between men and women for power, and the tensions within the family unit. The play ends with none of its conflicts resolved. Nowhere are the central obsessions of the Taylor canon—history, gender, and the family—brought together in a more disturbing way.

About a year after completing the play, at the urging of the editors of *The Kenyon Review*, Peter Taylor wrote a preface, which he describes as "a sort of history of the imaginary place and the imaginary people that I have here put together" (9). Called Faulknerian by Albert J. Griffith (rev. ed. 106), the piece certainly merits high praise, and it does bring to mind the opening pages of *The Hamlet* in which Faulkner sketches the early history of Frenchman's Bend. I would argue, however, that it is an even more memorable piece of writing in both its sweep and its texture. Take this passage in which Taylor presents the divergence of the early settlers of the play's "imaginary setting," Owl Mountain, from the contemporary pioneers of the lowlands:

> Life, instead of getting better for them after the first years, got worse. The early cabins they built might look very much like the early cabins built by the families who pushed on to the low country, but as the years went by the mountain man did not add to his cabin room after room, wing after wing

until the cabin had become something that could be called a Southern big house. Instead, the original log cabin on the Mountain generally deteriorated until it had to be abandoned—abandoned for a shanty-like structure with cheap siding from the saw mill, a tin roof that would soon rust out and have to be patched with flattened tin cans, and a jointed stovepipe in place of the old rock chimney. Though here and there one of the old cabins remains to this day, preserved by chance or by the assiduous attentions of some particularly industrious family, for the most part the only signs left of these cabins are the crumbling stone chimneys or chimney bases that one stumbles upon when hunting or fishing or picnicking. (10–11)

What rich suggestions of historical process, of economics and sociology, all conveyed through a vivid awareness of architecture.

The preface so obviously gives the play added resonance that producers and would-be producers have sought ways to bring it into the production of the play itself, one solution being to provide a narrator to speak sections of the text as prologue. The full preface, however, does not have a simple relationship to the play because it goes far afield at the same time that it provides an enriching frame for the work. A part of Taylor's impulse here is simply pleasure in capturing the history and spirit of a loved place—the old resort at Monteagle, Tennessee, which under different names appears in various works, including one of his most recent stories, "The Witch of Owl Mountain Springs." In the preface, an acute appreciation of the texture of history is tied to a deep understanding of historical process and of the roles of geography, economics, and racial character in forming the two groups inhabiting Monteagle or Owl Mountain—the mountain people and the summer people from the lowlands. This stimulating endeavor in historiography contains some of Peter Taylor's most insightful social commentary, and the historical impulse takes him considerably beyond the world of the play.

In tracing the history of the group to which the lowland cottage owners of Owl Mountain belong, he in fact most memorably defines the primary social subjects of his entire canon:

They are not, to be sure, ne'er-do-well, down-at-the-heel, old-line Southern gentry. Yet they are figuratively, and in many cases literally, the first cousins or even the brothers and sisters of that well-known breed. They have the same names as those you will find lingering in the old homeplaces in the lowlands. But they are the sons and daughters of the old regime who have had too much energy, too much vitality to be willing to accept shabby gentility as the way of life for the women or—for the men—either the frustrations of idleness or the dwindling rewards for farming or for practicing law in a country town. They are for the most part those whose forebears left the land a generation or so ago, and with their good names and their connections and their natural endowments went to the new Southern cities and towns to make a place for themselves. (17)

But if one impulse apparent in the preface is to go beyond the play (whether to detail architectural development, the influence of the Chautauqua movement, the shifting positions of various Protestant sects, or the social history of the South), another impulse brings Taylor back to the framing function. For his focus in *A Stand in the Mountains* is on a subgroup within the larger group defined above. He presents his cottage owners as those successful Southerners living just like others in the cities and suburbs of modern America but still retaining a fondness for the "old patterns of existence." For them Owl Mountain suggests the "old order of life." Taylor presents them as a "class unto themselves" (18). And just as this dowdy, old-fashioned resort owes its existence to the fact that it provided a refuge from the yellow fever epidemics that scourged the lowlands in the nineteenth century, so it now offers the nostalgic city-bred summer people "a retreat from the fever of modern life" (18).

History has, finally, brought confusion, fever. Thus, the preface points us toward the play. Although various characters display an awareness of the many complications of history, the major issue seems, at first, to be the change in gender roles effected by time. But one soon realizes that this is just one theme within a work suffused with questions of sex. And many of the issues of both gender and sexuality lead ultimately to matters of role and power in family relationships. Peter Taylor has a dialectical imagination, and nowhere is that more clearly demonstrated than in *A Stand in the Mountains*. Whereas some of the tensions dramatized here seem historical, others are apparently primal and thus timeless. One finds a clear and simple analysis of cause and effect often impossible. Like some other work of Peter Taylor's maturity, the play can be judged as either richly complex or frustratingly incohesive, but it is clearly anything but a seamless whole.

Taylor's dramatis personae are members of the Weaver family and those most closely connected with them. At the head of the family is Louisa Weaver, the aging but beautiful longtime widow of a Louisville corporation lawyer. The daughter of a poor Methodist preacher from a small west Tennessee town, Louisa has relished her career as a leader of society and taken vicarious pleasure in bringing a series of provincial young girls out in Louisville and thus launching their social careers. A person of intelligence, charm, and power of personality, she has also proved to be a castrating mother to her two sons. Harry, the older son now thirty, married a mountain girl when he was nineteen. To break away from his engulfing mother and her milieu, he attempted an escape into the past, as represented in the simple lives of the mountain folk. But the old cultural patterns, and especially the primitive gender roles, have failed to offer him sustenance. At the time the play opens, he has turned his hopes from past to future, to the world of inexorable change. The younger son, the would-be poet Zack, just returned from eight years in Europe, maintains an ironic distance from life, this detachment manifested in both his failure to write poetry of any real power and his inability to form any meaningful relationship with a woman.

Completing the gallery of males in the play is the boys' uncle (and Louisa's brother-in-law) Will Weaver, a weak surrogate father to the boys, a devoted platonic admirer of Louisa, a man romantically absorbed in regional history. The other women in *A Stand in the Mountains* are Harry's wife; her grandmother, Thelma Campbell; and two Weaver cousins. Georgia Morris, wealthy from three marriages, is a cousin who twenty years before disappointed Louisa by eloping with a worthless rich man immediately before her Louisville debut. Now playing at being a ceramist, she has dallied with Zack in Italy and come to the mountain to meet him and work in the native clay. Mina, the other cousin, is the prospective debutante of the moment, staying with Louisa in order to plan for the coming season.

Because of her success as a social leader and her association with the most anachronistic of gendered institutions, the debut, Louisa Weaver at first seems the character least aware of and least bothered by changes in the social order. But like the male Weavers, she too is sensitive to her own failure to respond effectively to new times. "One is born into a situation in life and by the time one has adjusted to it and made the best of it," she says, "the situation has altered entirely." Her next remarks, however, reflect the side of her nature that attracts so many people to her: "But one has to go on living, and caring about life, and enjoying the promises that are fulfilled even though they may be meaningless. And caring about life and enjoying it ultimately means caring about people and enjoying them" (69). Despite the powerful surrounding uncertainties, Louisa's core of surety and affirmation is characteristic, though sometimes in weaker measure, of the two younger women as well.

These three women are all stronger and more stable than the three Weaver men. Harry can present himself to his brother and uncle as a man of purpose. The disillusionment resulting from his immersion in mountain culture has brought him now, he maintains, "to want the things that most other people want" (52). Rejecting his wistful essay into the long hunter past for a chamber-of-commerce vision of the future, he is leading a movement to incorporate the village and the resort grounds in order to increase pressure on the state government to bring a new four-lane highway over Owl Mountain. He will open the mountain to the future and to prosperity. But his actual insecurity and, finally, his desperation become apparent during the long conversation with Mina in the third scene. She displays an openness to life and an appreciation of its variety, while at the same time being devoted to establishing an advantageous position for herself. In response to her vitality, flexibility, and frankness, he finally pours out his bitterness over desperate choices, admitting that he can't bear the sight of his wife and that "it's all over for me here. . . . I'm cornered. . . . All I can do is pull it down around me. Incorporate Owl Mountain! Bring the highway through" (67).

He leaves, and within minutes the play changes from what has seemed a Chekovian study of ineptitude and helplessness before change to a piece of Ibsen-like fissures and terrors. In the midst of a scene involving Louisa Weaver and her former and present protégés in which we get a glimpse of the choices offered women of a certain class over a couple of generations comes a startling scream and the sound of a shot. Within moments, old Mrs. Campbell enters with the bitter news that Harry has shot his wife, her granddaughter. The scene ends with Louisa Weaver's cry, "What has happened to us?" (73).

The violence that has erupted offstage is a measure of the sense of chaos that increasingly menaces the world of the play. But when the next scene opens, at first it appears that a kind of stability and order have been reestablished. The shooting, now three weeks past, has been accepted by many as an accident, and we learn that Harry, after his release from jail, has faithfully attended his invalid wife, spending much time reading to her from Uncle Will's histories. While others act to minimize effects, however, the injured woman's grandmother moves through the Weaver cottage, a disturbing choric figure, muttering of the acts of violence that both men and women have long committed in order to become disentangled from each other. A thunderstorm begins to build outside the cottage, and it is paralleled by mounting tensions within as the three Weaver men begin to drink and talk, arguing first among themselves before settling on "the real enemy": women (85). As the drunken talk intensifies, all three are lowered to their basic maleness. They may agree that women are "all bitches," but their responses to both of the young lowland women, Georgia and Mina, show how strongly the men are bound by lust (88). By the end of the scene, all three have revealed an underlying swinishness.

The first movement of the next scene functions as counterpoint and parallel. The drunken men, described by Louisa as "three mad bulls," are now either sleeping or away from the cottage. Mina has returned to the mountain from a visit to her home, where she was sent immediately after the shooting, and her reunion with Louisa complements the preceding scene of male bonding. "It's so stupid being a woman, Cousin Louisa; surely it wasn't always so. Surely it won't always be so." Mina thus expresses her own very modern confusion. Earlier both women have recognized men as, in a sense, the enemy, and now Mina muses, "Wouldn't it be wonderful if you didn't have to fit men into the picture" (90). But she goes on to admit that for her that is an impossible option. Georgia joins the other two women, and her remarks increase the sense of confusion over gender, role, and an era of change. She also brings the conversation to the matter of sex, revealing that she and Harry have been having an affair since the shooting. It is clear now that both younger women are drawn to Harry despite themselves, and both hope that he is successful in that day's election on the issue of incorporating the village. Here this very complicated scene turns. The rest of the dialogue among the three women is punctuated by conflicting reports of the election results and the sound from the next room of the now imperious invalid mountain wife calling for her husband. Finally, Harry enters the cottage with the news that the vote is almost unanimously against incorporation. Seething with the knowledge that his wife and her grandmother have secretly led a campaign against him to gain their vengeance, he leaves the living room to answer the commands of the imperious voice.

Sounds of violent struggle are heard offstage, and Harry, scratched and bloody, stumbles through the living room and out the front door. Zack goes to the bedroom and finds Harry's wife dead, her neck broken. In the next short scene, the stunned group at the Weaver cottage learns that Harry has gone to his own house, where he has shot and killed his two small sons and his wife's grandmother before turning the gun on himself.

The final scene serves as coda. It opens with the introduction of two important images. Will Weaver gives to Zack the ancient limestone knife that Harry and Will had found years before and that Will has kept as a treasured artifact. The giving of the knife is followed by a report of news from the Nashville paper that the highway is indeed coming over Owl Mountain and directly through the village. Influenced perhaps by this juxtaposition of images—knife and highway, past and future—Will Weaver lapses into nostalgic ramblings. "We're Lee in the mountains," Zack comments, bringing to the surface the issue buried beneath his uncle's ramblings (107). The cottage owners of Owl Mountain, Zack is saying, are trying to escape modern confusion and change for a moment, to rally their resources, to connect past with present, to make a last stand—just as Lee was urged to do at the end of the Civil War. But in answer to Zack's subsequent question as to what's gone wrong with the country, Will can only reply that it might be enough to understand simply what's gone wrong with one's self. What follows is another of the startling moments of the play. Will reveals that he has never slept with a woman. Rather than being any sort of surrogate father to the Weaver sons, then, Uncle Will has simply been another brother, loving their mother as a child would. He has failed as a man in both love and work, seeking in the first an escape from maturity and in the second an escape from time. The revelation is startling because it shifts our attention so abruptly from the issues of history and change to the question of primal patterns of sexuality and family structure.

Now remains only the final leave-taking. Zack is departing the mountain for, in his words, "[O]ne place or another" (110). He has found no sense of place and no sense of purpose or identity. Louisa and Will are not going back to Louisville in the winter, but they are remaining on the mountain, retreating at least for a while. Mina is staying for a few months to be near Louisa. The play ends on a muted note, with Mina encouraging Louisa's plans to remodel the cottage, at least an incipient sign of a returning engagement in life. But the final darkness that falls on the stage contributes to the somber feeling of the end.

Just what are we to make of *A Stand in the Mountains*? A product of the historical moment at which it was written, the late 1960s, when the social fabric of America seemed to many to be coming apart, is the play intended basically to give us a sense of the confusion of a time in which causes and effects were difficult to separate and identify? Is that the reason for Taylor's shifting back and forth here among central themes without always suggesting satisfactory causal connection? If so, he often succeeds brilliantly on this mimetic level.

One can also see the play, however, as reflecting a movement away from the unifying impulse itself. On the one hand, much of the confusion and suffering can be traced to the inexorable driving force of history, as reflected so well by the image of the highway. On the other hand, much of the dilemma of the Weaver family can be traced to a cause that is in no way time bound—the lack of that sexual balance that is essential to the health of the family unit. That theme is suggested by the image of the ancient phallic knife, especially in the last scene as we see the artifact passed from one impotent male to another.

Early in the very first scene, Zack's ironic allusion to his parents' "bedchamber" points us to the sexual center of the family (24). The absence of the father and therefore of sexual balance within the unit has resulted in an enmeshed family, dominated by a powerful mother whom her sons both desire and feel threatened by. The younger son, though sexually capable, is ultimately as impotent as his uncle (and false surrogate father) in his lack of engagement with life. The older son, whose virility attracts all the sexually active women in the play, is never able to find balance and fulfillment in the expression of his manhood. His masculinity can finally express itself only through violence.

It is interesting to discover that Taylor is subtly playing with both axes of the play even in the preface. Although that text is fundamentally concerned with the process of change through time, here Taylor has also embedded the recurrent image of lovers, most often lovers amid ruins. From the beginning, then, for readers of the play, the motifs of both history and sex have been sounded.

The notes recur throughout the play without ever quite merging. In *A Stand in the Mountains,* as in so many of Taylor's most memorable texts, there is something that works against closure, that keeps the text open, and sends the reader back through the pages for answers. But again, though historical process and matters of primal sexuality seem most often dual, sometimes alternative, axes of the play, one can almost see how at points, buried beneath all the layered concerns of the text, one axis comes near reflecting the other.

If the play is basically concerned, as I believe it is, with the death of the patriarchal order, then there is often a symbolic mirroring by the family of the larger social world, and the play possesses that allegorical dimension that marks much of Taylor's most powerful fiction. ("Miss Leonora When Last Seen," "Venus, Cupid, Folly and Time," and "In the Miro District" are particularly good examples.) Obviously the play is set in a world without a center, or at one of those Yeatsian points where the center cannot hold. No one knows quite what to believe in. Georgia remarks that the "mountain people, and Owl Mountain itself" are Harry's "God" (99). But we see how tenuously he holds to them. All other central beliefs or obsessions are shown as equally hollow or destructive. Of his devotion to writing the history of the mountain, Uncle Will admits finally, "My work is my sickness" (109). He has sought escape to the past in order to avoid the central issues of existence. Zack and his uncle are left musing at the end on "What went wrong" with both "old America" and "one's self" (108). We are given in the play a confused world that is reflected in a confused family. Just as the root cause of the social chaos is the lack of a controlling center, so can the root cause of the family dilemma be traced to the absence of the father.

Both Louisa's last name, "Weaver," and our first sight of her working with her needle repairing Oriental rugs underscore the suggestion that she is an aging Penelope, as do her son's reactions to her suitors. In the sons, Taylor has given us two contemporary Telemachuses. Both are seekers. Neither has a guide. Neither can achieve a satisfying male role.

In its treatment of the patriarchal order, the play also occupies a significant place in Taylor's canon. Looking at the career from one angle, one can argue that Taylor's primary subject from the beginning has been the patriarchy, the roles offered within the order, the consequences of its breaking up. It is now a commonplace in Taylor criticism that much of the best of his earliest fiction dealt with the place of women within such a traditionally ordered society. Even the title of Taylor's first mature story, "A Spinster's Tale," published in 1940, reflects that emphasis. Perhaps the earliest important story to treat the problems and abuses of the system, with men as the focus, is "Porte-Cochere," published in 1949. That work was strikingly anomalous when first collected in a volume whose title well reflected its emphasis on women, *The Widows of Thornton* (1954). *A Stand in the Mountains* comes at that moment when Taylor was turning from women to men as his primary subjects. The play itself virtually reenacts the shift in emphasis, perhaps a reflection of its long gestation and the various drafts and forms it underwent. Taylor's initial conception was a prose piece devoted to a figure like Louisa Weaver and titled "The Girl from Forked Deer"; and Louisa, indeed, is the figure of most compelling interest at the beginning of the play. She almost drops out, however, during the second half, and her sons emerge as hauntingly dysfunctional characters.

Jane Barnes Casey's important 1978 essay, which was the first to note Taylor's shift from female to male subjects, argues that that change is reflected most dramatically in the 1977 collection *In the Miro District and Other Stories*. But the shift begins earlier. I locate it in 1968 and 1969, as manifested in *A Stand in the Mountains* and in the last two stories Taylor published before bringing out *The Collected Stories* in 1969: "Dean of Men" and "First Heat," both works concerned with the issue of manhood. The next volume after *Collected Stories* was *Presences* (1973), which collected seven one-act plays, more markedly violent and in general more sexually explicit than anything Taylor had written, though most would agree not Taylor's best work. These lines of development lead to *In the Miro District,* Taylor's favorite volume (Robison 144) and many critics would argue his most powerful—marked by powerful, disturbing images and centered on men.

One watches the entire line of development begin in *A Stand in the Mountains.* It is a central text in the Taylor canon, one that cannot be ignored in any study of Taylor's obsessive themes—history, gender, and family. The play retained a peculiar fascination for Peter Taylor. In the fall of 1993, he began working on a novel based on *A Stand in the Mountains,* using Zack as the first-person narrator. The working title is *Call Me Telemachus* (personal interview, 10 Aug. 1993).

Peter Taylor's "The Old Forest"

ANN BEATTIE

IN THE HANDS of a lesser talent, Peter Taylor's story "The Old Forest" might be primarily a social history of a particular place in the South at a particular time: history and sociology dovetailed to produce a sort of essay on manners and mores (of course, with farther reaching significance, if the writer was delicate enough to persuade and smart enough to intuit the metaphors inherent in the terrain, as Peter Taylor is). Yet in spite of almost copious information about the Memphis of 1937—descriptions constantly dropped in by the narrator to interrupt the narrative, to inform the reader of Memphis's past, and to point the way, by story's end, to an understanding of the Memphis of the future, I doubt that the story strikes anyone as primarily a social essay animated by fictional characters. Rather, it is a complex, entirely convincing work of fiction that happens to veer off course quite often. Ostensibly, this is to enable context to provide a necessary perspective on the characters' actions. I say "ostensibly" because Peter Taylor is a gratifyingly sneaky writer.

Almost anyone who has tried to write any story knows there is a gap—sometimes a wider gap than the writer sees, alas—between what is known inside the writer's head and what gets communicated on the page. Often a few added lines can anticipate or explain unintentional confusions, but in other cases, friends' and editors' perplexed expressions as they flip backward in the text tell you immediately you've gone wrong, somewhere. Usually, you want your story to have a clear trajectory: after all, most readers will only follow a guide whose voice has authority. If you are convinced enough yourself, as the writer, readers will even follow you over the edge of the cliff—or a high enough percentage of them will. This has its advantages, because once you have launched them into the ecstatic Jules-and-Jim or Thelma-and-Louise limbo, anything goes. You will have less trouble convincing people of your authority midair than at their point of departure, on the ground. Some writers are simply good at entrapment. Others are genuinely bullish. But whether writers seduce readers through grace or sheer force of insistence, readers have to be trapped. Quite simply, they cannot be allowed to get up and walk around the room because what they see—whatever story is going on in the room—will distract them from *your* story, your made-up story, the story you have been compelled to tell. There are almost as many approaches to cornering the reader as there are writers. They include writing so beautiful that tone and content alone conspire to captivate the reader's attention (the first sentence of Don De-Lillo's *Libra*). Or they pull out all the stops and plunge the reader into the unfamiliar (many of Donald Barthelme's uniquely brilliant stories). Then there are writers who advance and retreat, charge and feint, athletes who elicit energy by creating energy themselves, and who maintain momentum by switching gears—or, to keep with my metaphor, by playing basketball until it suddenly seems advantageous to play hockey. Then Merlin-like, they deflate the basketball to a small puck and send it sailing across the ice.

You may be initially surprised to know that I think Peter Taylor is one of the athletes. A philosopher athlete, to be sure, but a real master of possibilities, a writer so sure of timing and trajectory, so able to sense the inevitable form of his complex story, that he cannot resist setting an obstacle course for himself, and for us, by complicating the process.

"The Old Forest" exists and deepens in meaning on so many levels that if it were not so action packed, reading it would be like considering an enormous slag of sedimentary rock. It has been layered so the central event of the story (a car accident that takes place shortly before Nat's, the narrator's, marriage) leaves us with an image of footsteps in the snow, left by Lee Ann Deehart (a friend who was with him when the accident occurred—not Nat's fiancée) as she flees the scene of the accident.

When Lee Ann runs away, the demands on the reader increase: the reader is bifurcated into the character who takes flight and the character who remains, shaken and slightly injured. Larger than either character, though—larger than life—are those footsteps in the snow, which begin to intensify as the story progresses, becoming, in effect, more noticeable each time the snowfall deepens. (Nat tells us: "I didn't even know she was out of the car until I got around on the other side and saw the door there standing open and saw her tracks in the snow, going down the bank" [*OF* 40].) As long as Lee Ann is on the run, we too are in a suspended state, but because we know nothing of where she has gone, we stay tentatively at Nat's side, allied with our only remaining guide. As we read, it seems that what transpired is simply being reported: there was an accident; Lee Ann ran from the car and disappeared; Nat is left to ponder what happened. Though the actual narrative of the story happens long after the events, Nat nevertheless chooses to string us along—to create a mystery story, interspersed with much information about the history of the place. Had Peter Taylor decided to have the young Nat as narrator—had the story been told from a young man's vantage point—we might not hear as much as we do about such things as the "giant oak and yellow poplar trees older than the memory of the earliest white settler" (38) simply because such diction would be strange for a young person and because a young person would probably not be inclined to digress in such a way when telling a story. Tension increases each time the plot is interrupted, following the mysterious disappearance, as Nat offers information about the forest out of which Memphis was settled. Along with everything else they represent and symbolize, the woods—we gradually come to see—begin to stand for our own confusion, our own dark lack of knowing. We are frightened when Nat recalls that long ago women who wanted to escape the harm of so-called civilization ran into the woods, upset to be reminded that Indians who lurked in the woods were known to mutilate their victims. But because Nat so often succeeds in upsetting us, a sort of simultaneity of time is created, in which the present seems not so far from the past, and vice versa. Logic tells us that if Lee Ann was seen by skaters and by a truck driver, and that if she "traveled at a remarkable speed" (40), she probably knew where she was going, and she is all right. But emotionally, she could not be doing well—which we gradually come to understand as the story progresses. Only when she is gone do we have reason to stand in judgment of Nat. Her footsteps break not only the surface of the snow, but the surface of life in Memphis, whited-out by what is seldom said (that girls of a particular class are fine for fun, but not for marrying). If "The Old Forest" had only been a story about Nat and Lee Ann, narrated by the young Nat, we would never have gotten to know them—and even when we do, it is by reading between the lines and by intuiting, as the characters must, what is left unsaid in the all-too-socially-correct silences.

It is also the presence of Nat's fiancée, Caroline Braxley, who, at age nineteen, clearly has more wisdom than Nat, who forces the issue to be confronted, as together they set out to solve the mystery of Lee Ann's disappearance. Although Nat receives anonymous phone calls telling him to stop pursuing Lee Ann (the reader wonders if he wouldn't, in fact, easily forget her if other people in the community were not forcing him to find her), and though he talks to some of her closed-mouthed friends, it is not until he and Caroline meet Nat's ex-lover, Fern, that they (and we) get a clue. It is interesting to realize that Fern's name offers a subtle link with the forest—and also interesting to notice that in a photograph that provides the clue to Lee Ann's disappearance, Lee Ann is described standing with a woman, who turns out to be her grandmother, "in one of the flower beds against the side of the house" (78). Time after time, though it is always subtly done (much is made by Nat of Caroline's tallness; she is at one point described by Nat as "willowy"), the women are connected with the natural order, the "good" forest, whereas Nat assumes that the world is interesting only in hierarchical, historical terms or hypnotizes us by conjuring up the scary fairy-tale aspects of the forest, asking us to see it much the way Longfellow lushly described it in the preface to "Evangeline" ("the primeval forest," Nat calls it—lest we miss its archetypal significance). We also learn, in Nat's almost endlessly informative narrative, that the forest "has only recently been saved by a very narrow margin of a great highway that men wished to put through there—saved by groups of women determined to save this last bit of the old forest from the axes of modern man" (53). Simply put, Nat is wary of the ancient, dark, chaotic forest that some would call chthonian, yet knows that the women in his life are drawn to its interior.

In the course of the narrative, we come to understand that Nat is quite reticent to enter the forest. But without going into the forest—literally and symbolically—what does Nat have? Although the story is also old, like the forest, before it is told (Nat's narrative transpires when he is in his sixties), he seems, strangely, not to have a great deal more insight into the human condition than he did when he was a young man. Not far into the story, he drops in the information that many tragedies have befallen him. In fact, they are rather extensive tragedies: the horrible deaths of both parents, the premature deaths of two of his own children, his brothers' deaths in the Korean war. Before mentioning these tragedies, he remarks, "In a way, it is strange that I remember all these impressions [of Lee Ann and the accident] so vividly after forty years, because it is not as though I have lived an uneventful life during the years since" (42). Strange, and not so strange, the reader realizes. In the post-Freudian world, we take for granted that those things that are sublimated and unarticulated are the most troubling. There are certainly times when Nat all but admits his cowardice in many things, including his not marrying Lee Ann. But even if he does not see—which is doubtful, though his intent to disguise becomes predictable—then still the reader gradually comes to realize what he does not. A simple Freudian-based assessment of Nat would hardly be to the point, though, and to paraphrase Nat-the-narrator, Memphis in 1937 must certainly reverberate with a deeper significance than just the fact that such was life in Memphis circa 1937.

Much has been made, with good reason, of Chekhov as a precedent for Peter Taylor's art. In *A Summons to Memphis,* and in "The Old Forest" as well, I suspect that a bit of Ford Madox Ford has also been mixed in because—as with Edward Ashburnham in *The Good Soldier*—we must increasingly suspect that we are being told a story by a somewhat unreliable narrator. So good is Peter Taylor at giving us a narrator through whose eyes the world springs alive that, as the author, he all but manages to obscure the obvious about his character: he is a narrator who sees subjectively, and at least as narrowly as he suspects, if not more so, and the truth of the situation, and therefore of his life, may be quite antithetical to his presentation. Some of what he says, in part because of the sheer quantity of his revelations, might better be considered as a distracting preemptive strike, rather than forthrightness. It is difficult not to think that Nat protests a bit too much in such statements as, "I think that, besides its coming at that impressionable period of my life and the fact that one just does remember things better from one's youth, there is the undeniable fact that life *was* different in those times" (42). It serves Nat well to think so; otherwise, his deficiencies might become painfully clear. This is, after all, a man who would not get off the road when another vehicle was headed toward him because that vehicle was not supposed to be there.

As Nat lists the tragedies of his life, it is difficult to believe that the after-effects of all of them could have been so subdued by time that they could emerge, as they do, as a mere list—and an almost parenthetical one at that. Although he invokes the social hierarchy of Memphis in his attempt to present himself as part of the status quo, Nat is actually more unusual than he realizes, blunted in some way so that whereas with some people things go unspoken (his father, his fiancée, her parents), he would have us think that with him, they even go *unthought*. Only infrequently, as if to outguess the reader's possible question, does he confront the subtext of the situation. And if we have been lulled by what an authority figure he seems, and what a good storyteller he is—if we have not paid careful attention—then we have missed the essential clue to his personality. At one point, he announces that Lee Ann was the catalyst for this realization: "I felt that I had never looked at her really or had any conception of what sort of person she was or what her experience in life was like. Now it seemed I would never know. I suddenly realized—at that early age—that there was experience to be had in life that I might never know anything about except through hearsay and through books. I felt that this was my last moment to reach out and understand something of the world that was other than my own narrow nature" (79–80). Indeed, in later life Nat repudiates the family business to become a teacher, though his almost militant obtuseness can only lead us to wonder what he derived from his reading, and his inflectionlessly stated "tragedies" make one wonder how his actions might ever change, even if his life began to transpire in a new context. Although he finds himself commendable, it seems an understatement to say that he remains conservative to a fault.

"The Old Forest" seems to me to be about the road not taken—perhaps because it was seen by a particular character as being only a road (whose history was known, so that certain facts could be recited about the bends and valleys). From the snowy, hidden road Nat and Lee Ann drive on early, we move through time to a "three lane strip of concrete" (83)—the new world versus the old, brilliantly and shockingly described as Nat suddenly looks in his rearview mirror and we see, along with him, the direction civilization is inevitably taking. Although Nat says, "It was not clear to me immediately what there was in that skyline to inspire all that followed" (84–85) (when Caroline has an outburst), the reader cannot help but feel that unlike Nat, Caroline does not need to rely on externals to speak. She has a passion he lacks, an ability to cut to the heart of the problem (Lee Ann has a heart: she's Deehart), even a strategy for saving herself—thereby saving (such as anyone could) Nat. As she expresses her frustration with the way society operates, as she speaks openly and honestly about what has happened to someone who seems not quite to know, she and Nat pass a sign it must have delighted Peter Taylor to include: "Speed Limit: Please Drive Carefully." As if no one would disobey sensible rules. As if order could be maintained. In fact, I think Peter Taylor has shown us that it can, if one is willing to pay a great price.

Lee Ann's spontaneous run leads her to an awareness of what action she needs to take—what she needs to do to restore herself, to live honestly. But at the end of the story she is absent—as she has so often been absent—and we are left with another problematic situation—that might even be called another tragedy, of sorts: Nat and Caroline, on the same metaphorical road, yet miles apart in sensibility, speeding past the sign, heading, as we all are, toward journey's end. Though Nat marries a woman whose mind races ahead of his, the only speed he ever musters is behind the wheel of his car (at her request). Paradoxically, though Nat drives ninety miles an hour, he is sadly slow in everything. It is only slowly—more than forty years elapse between the events and their telling—that Nat speaks, and when he does, his deep desire seems to be to cover his own footprints. Like everyone else caught up in a mystery, though, he leaves clues. And if the drift of his intentionally persuasive words does not fill in those tracks, the reader will see more clearly than he the sad truth about the narrow path he has chosen.

Memory, Rewriting, and the Authoritarian Self in *A Summons to Memphis*

ROBERT H. BRINKMEYER, JR.

Peter taylor has frequently talked about the cognitive value of writing. "I think writing fiction is a cognitive instrument," he told Wendy Smith in a 1985 interview. "You learn what you really think from what you write" (63). A few years later, in an interview with Barbara Thompson, he commented more fully: "I think trying to write is a religious exercise. You are trying to understand life, and you can only get the illusion of doing it fully by writing. That is, it's the only way I can come to understand things fully. When I create, when I put my own mark on something and form it, I begin to know the whole truth about it, how it was put together. . . . [Writing] is making sense of life. It is coming to understand yourself" (158–59).

"Making sense of life" and "coming to understand yourself" meant most immediately for Taylor exploring one's memories—not merely remembering but reshaping and recasting one's memories in an ongoing quest not for fact but for meaning. In this regard, Taylor shared much with Katherine Anne Porter, a writer whom he deeply admired; in his interview with Thompson, Taylor said that what he loved about Porter was that "she managed to interpret the events of her life in her stories, just by writing them down" (159). Like Porter, Taylor did not write strictly autobiographical stories, but instead revised and altered event and situation, transforming what Porter liked to call "adventure" into "experience" (Porter 92). As Porter underscores in her essay "St. Augustine and the Bullfight," engaging one's memories breaks down the cherished notions of self that a person typically hides behind, freeing one from the authoritative self's stranglehold. For Porter, the temptation for the artist was to write entirely by the vision of the authoritarian self, repressing the liberating challenges of memory. Taylor in all likelihood would find little to disagree with in Porter's characterization of artistic creation as an ongoing rereading and rewriting of the past to destabilize the authoritarian self, a process of "endless remembering" in which "events are changed, reshaped, interpreted again and again in different ways" (468).

"Endless remembering" might also characterize the musings of Phillip Carver, the narrator of *A Summons to Memphis,* who pores over his past in an effort to understand himself and his family. Although Carver is not an artist attempting to write fiction, his descent into memory bears striking resemblance to Taylor's (and Porter's) conception of artistic endeavor. His narrative is anything but straight recall; rather it is a tortured and tortuous act of interpretation, a reading of the past by the writing of it. Necessarily repetitive in places, Carver's narrative circles around a few key events and characters, testing and retesting formulations to explain their significance. This retrospective narrative framework, in which the story told by the narrator is complicated, as David M. Robinson puts it, by an awareness "that his telling of the story must also be an act of interpretation and self-comprehension" (56), is a signature of Taylor's fiction. As in Faulkner's *Absalom, Absalom!* the focus in *Summons* is less on *what* happened in the past than on the narrator's attempt in the present to explain *why* things happened in the past—and then how and why the narrator interprets as he does. Most of the suspense in *Summons* thus involves not the story Phillip tells but the way he tells it. "Each page seems to hold out the promise that Phillip is about to frame a memory in a way that might free him from his aloofness," Ann Hulbert observes (67), and one question that looms at the end is whether Phillip ever achieves this breakthrough. Looming, too, is the question of how good a reader Phillip is of his own narrative. What, in other words, does Phillip learn in telling his story?

The kernel of Phillip's narration is the events ensuing from his sisters' asking him to return to Memphis to help prevent their father from remarrying. These events, as becomes almost immediately clear as Phillip tells his story, have forced him to confront his decidedly conflicted feelings about his father and his family—and finally about himself. The more Phillip says, the wider expand the horizons of his tale; as he explicitly comments in several places, the simple events about which he speaks can be understood only in the context of what has happened long before, not merely in his own life, but in the lives of all the people who are involved. What begins as a fairly detached commentary on how grown-up children in Memphis customarily seek to prevent widowed fathers from remarrying becomes in short order a complex and convoluted meditation on self and world, or perhaps better, self-in-world. In an interview with J. William Broadway, Taylor identified "the most important thing in serious fiction" as "the relationship of character to setting, if you will, or to the world or to the context of their lives" (83), and certainly it is Phillip's relationship with the context of his life that is most important in *Summons*. The context of Phillip's life is best understood as the people with whom he interacts, particularly his father, who most influenced him growing up, and Holly Kaplan, who is closest to him in his adult life. Phillip's interactions with these people, together with those with his sisters and Alex Mercer, coalesce into a coherent pattern that, as David M. Robinson has observed, reveals both Phillip's "gradual and positive coming to terms with the causes of the 'ruin' of his life and the exposure of [him] as a weak and passionless phantom" (55).

Up until the time that he begins to think back over his past after being called to Memphis, Phillip has always seen his father as an authoritarian tyrant, a man who ruled his family with an iron grip. During his upbringing, Phillip characterized his father as "a barrier between me and any independent life I might aspire to—a barrier to any pursuit of ideas, interests, goals that my temperament guided me toward"(*SUM* 74). Phillip's characterization of his father as a "barrier" suggests the rage for order that he sees driving his father, manifested most obviously in his obsessive desire to wall the family off from the rest of the world in order to maintain the security he enjoys as patriarch of the family. It seems to Phillip that his father can survive the disorder of the fast-changing times, exemplified most crushingly in the financial scandal he is caught up in, only by dictatorially demanding that the family order remain intact, with everyone following his commands with absolute allegiance. Thus Phillip's thoughts about the motives underlying his father's decision to move the family to Memphis: "He could only have the strength to start over if he felt he had lost nothing of himself, if he was certain that all his dependents were still his dependents. No one must be allowed to defect or he would feel that he was not entering whole into the life ahead of him. Something like that, I think. He did enter so, and perhaps that *is* what sustained him in the years immediately afterward, sustained *him* and in some degree destroyed the rest of us" (36). As his final words here suggest, Phillip sees his father as utterly selfish, concerned only with his own success and blind to the havoc he wreaks upon the family in seeking it. Phillip goes on to develop a strong case against his father for the damage he has inflicted: his mother's inability to adapt to Memphis life and her subsequent retreat into invalidism; his brother Georgie's determined escape from his father's authoritarianism to fight, and die doing so, the much more evil authoritarianism of the Nazis; his sisters' emotional stunting that leaves them frozen in the role of vengeful adolescents after their father torpedoes their chances at marriage; and Phillip's own emotional stunting (that the reader recognizes even if Phillip does not always) that sours him into cynicism and aloofness, particularly after his father covertly undermines his relationship with Clara Price.

Phillip's reading of his father's authoritarian use of power ironically mirrors Phillip's own authoritarian control of his memories of his father; his reading of his father, blaming him for all of the family's problems, frees Phillip from any responsibility and is the "barrier" that keeps him cut off from any deep communion with his father. It is Phillip's authoritarian control of his father's past—the temptation of the monologic artist—that comes under severe testing when he begins to think back on his life after his sisters call him to return home to prevent his father's remarriage. The disjointed movement of his musings, with one association giving way to others and so preventing neat and simple resolutions, itself suggests the complexity of the issues he ponders and calls into question his straightforward reading of the family's past that he heretofore has thoughtlessly accepted. This undoing is not lost on Phillip, who, as he tries to recount and explain, frequently admits how much he does not know and cannot adequately fathom, how many questions he still has, and how little his previous readings of his family's history make sense. At one point, for instance, after having worked through an analysis of the damage to the family's stability resulting from the move to Memphis, Phillip calls it all into question: "Perhaps, though, it wasn't the move at all. Perhaps we were something vestigial—as a family, as a class of people even. Perhaps it wasn't the move but only my father's insistence that the family should be moved intact, merely an expression of his need to have his wife and children with him, and with himself altogether unchanged, if he were to successfully begin his career over like a young man" (21). At another point, he admits how unsure he finally remains about his mother's transformation after moving to Memphis: "I don't know still whether the trauma of the move changed her or whether the move from Nashville to Memphis merely happened to coincide with alterations in her mood and character. Or it may be that at some time, perhaps several years past, she had reached the limits of her sympathetic nature, maybe that she was by nature a good mother to children so long as they *were* children but not after they became adolescents and grown-up children" (48).

Phillip's tortuous musings not only suggest his growing confusion but also, of more importance, point to his moving away from what we might call the authoritarian author (writing merely to justify one's already held positions) to that of cognitive author (writing to test and challenge one's positions). He sees that he must fathom, rather than pigeonhole, his confusion if he is to come to any meaningful understanding of the past and of his feelings toward others. Most obviously signaling his growing maturity and insightfulness are the advances he makes in breaking the hold of his authoritarian perspective by detaching himself from it in his narration to see things from the perspective of others. Essentially aloof and disinterested and set in his comfortable routines, Phillip is not naturally given to such imaginative forays. In this he contrasts sharply with Alex Mercer, who by nature seems given to sympathetic understanding. As Phillip notes early on, Alex "employ[ed] his imagination in an almost literary way on everything and everybody he wishes to understand"; Phillip adds that in Alex's letters to him about his sisters, he always strived "to enter into their experience with all possible sympathy" (50). Rather than sympathizing with others, Phillip typically judges them from a high-minded position of authority and omniscience, as he does when he forthrightly declares that Alex's efforts to understand Phillip's sisters ultimately fail because his "provincial Memphis love for a *simple* truth" blinds him to the complex love/hate feelings Phillip declares they hold for their father. "About my sisters Alex certainly understood much less than I," he concludes (80). Alex, of course, is a much better reader of character and situation than Phillip gives him credit for; and, ironically, it is only when Phillip can become more like the sympathetic Alex, particularly with regard to his father, that he can be the knowing and loving son he has never been. (Alex, of course, has taken the role of dutiful son during Phillip's separation, psychological and otherwise, from his father.)

Becoming involved in the wranglings between his father and his sisters nudges Phillip progressively closer to a sympathetic understanding of his family, particularly his father. It is easy for Phillip to remain detached and judgmental toward his family when he lives in the sanctuary of his New York apartment (the authoritarian author); it is much less so when he is visiting in Memphis and has to deal with people face-to-face and work through his feelings toward them (the cognitive author). Spurring the breakdown of the psychological barriers that have kept him detached is his witnessing of his sisters' attempts to control the life of his father. If Phillip has been guardian of his father's past, his sisters now seek to control his present. Their manipulations of his life make up a rewritten version of his earlier manipulations. Mr. Carver had once attempted to keep the family intact and his place as patriarch secure; now Jo and Betsy attempt to cement the family together with him as patriarch, even though he is long past wanting this position. His children's courtings were sabotaged; now Mr. Carver's are. Jo and Betsy moved out of Mr. Carver's house; now they move back in. The two sisters arranged Phillip's departure to New York; now they call him back. There is more than concern about inheritance here; there is revenge. Taylor for a while had considered calling *Summons* "Vengeance Is Mine," but more appropriate would have been "Vengeance Is Ours" because Mr. Carver's overt antagonists are Jo and Betsy, not Phillip.

But, of course, Phillip's actions toward his father are far from innocent. His move to New York, for instance, a devastating blow to his father, seems to have been not only a step to gain personal freedom but also one to inflict suffering on his father. Moreover, when he returns to Memphis after his sisters' calls, Phillip's conflicted feelings toward his father, laced with a good deal of ill will, prevent him from actively supporting him in his attempts to live fully and happily. To his credit, Phillip can recognize the malice in his sisters' manipulation of their father's life; to his discredit, he cannot see his own and for the most part remains uninvolved, failing to take the kind of decisive step Alex Mercer hopes he will to help his father. If Phillip is not an active agent of evil here, he certainly is a passive one because his failure to act helps make evil actions by others possible.

Overcoming this hesitancy to rally to his father's aid involves Phillip's working through and recasting his feelings toward his father so as to achieve some type of sympathetic understanding of him; in other words, it involves rewriting his relationship with his father with the openness of a cognitive author. The progress toward this rewriting is slow-going, marked by fits and starts, with Phillip inching along, spurred every so often by sudden moments of imaginative insight that typically come when he reaches an understanding of his father through his own suffering. One such moment occurs when the piercing loneliness he feels when sitting alone in his apartment (Holly having moved out) prompts him to consider his father's isolation. His own fears of being alone shed light on what he understands must be his father's, and Phillip moves toward a deep, sympathetic identification that calls for active involvement in his father's affairs: "At any rate, I tried to see Father's surroundings now through his own eyes. And I was certain he was no less lonely than I for living surrounded by objects for which he had reverence and even genuine affection. His loneliness was perhaps even more profound just because of them. Identifying thus with Father, I resolved suddenly then to go back to the telephone and make reservations for my flight tomorrow morning. (It somehow always gave me extra energy to pretend I was really like my father. It did so even when I was a boy.) I resolved, moreover, to telephone him at once that I would be arriving" (130–31).

As with other moments when he sympathetically reads his father, Phillip's determination to act wholeheartedly on his behalf is short-lived; his underlying resentment quickly reasserts itself, and his authoritarian self regains control, smothering other, more sympathetic, views of Mr. Carver. Each instance of sympathetic rereading and rewriting, however, progressively undermines the power of his authoritarianism.

Even more helpful than his struggles with loneliness for prodding him to read his father sympathetically are his conversations with Holly after they are back together again, particularly those dealing with how adults should relate to their parents. In these talks Holly challenges Phillip to seek reconciliation through understanding, a challenge that essentially calls for him to downplay as wrong-headed the resentment toward his father that he has kept smoldering since adolescence. Phillip, in contrast, early on decides that the best way to overcome his resentment is to forget it by forgetting his father's wrongs. At one point, he writes that as an adolescent he should have voiced his anger at his father and then "have forgotten the whole business. But now, since I had not, it was the part of maturity to forget those old conflicts." He goes on to vow that he will protect his father from Jo and Betsy and then seek to convert his sisters to his view about forgetting parental wrongs: " 'Forget, forget,' I kept insisting silently, as if further to convince myself before confronting Betsy and Josephine. I resolved that my sisters must be made to accept my doctrine of forgetting. It was too late to forgive, of course. And vengeance was not the alternative" (134). A bit later, Phillip celebrates the power of forgetting and what he sees as his new maturity:

> [Forgetfulness] transcended all my many other feelings toward Father. The idea of forgetting all that I had ever held against him was like forgetting the cruelties of fate itself. And I took no credit for the willed act of forgetting. It was impossible to look upon the man's radiant face and not forget real or imagined injuries he had done me. At any rate, at this moment I went over again the profound generalization and truth that had dawned upon me earlier. Forgetting the injustices and seeming injustices which one suffered from one's parents during childhood and youth must be the major part of any maturing process. I kept repeating this to myself, as though it were a lesson I would at some future time be accountable for. A certain oblivion was what we must undergo in order to become adults and live peacefully with ourselves. (145–46)

If he is not exactly at peace with himself, Phillip's doctrine of forgetting his father's wrongs spurs him to remember other, more positive things about his father and to reconstruct what he knows about his early life with sympathetic understanding.

But is Phillip's way of forgetting finally the means to maturity? Is forgetting the best way for remembering? As almost everyone knows, it is next to impossible to succeed in willing oneself to forget something—the very act of willing involves the calling forth of the memory to be repressed, and there is always, too, the unexpected emergence of memories over which one has no control into the conscious mind. Phillip himself seems instinctively aware of the shortcomings of his position, even if he does not openly admit it; in the two passages just cited, he seems compelled continually to repeat to himself the validity of forgetting both to assure himself of his rightness and to keep control of his memories, as if he were chanting a mantra. Obviously, he cannot spend all his time in recitation; and recitation itself suggests the dead end that forgetting leads to for creative sympathy and creation—it is a closing rather than an opening up of self for imaginative understanding.

Certainly Holly understands the limits of Phillip's doctrine of forgetting, and she urges him to revise his position. Forgetting, she rightly points out to him during their many talks about their fathers, finally avoids the issue of one's feelings. She counsels Phillip to accept his father by understanding him, a position that at first glance seems similar to that of the cognitive artist. Phillip writes of her advice: "She wished me to do more than forget the old wrongs. She wished me to try to see him in a light that would not require either forgetting or forgiving. She frequently urged me to talk about him, as she certainly had not urged me to do in years, and to try to give her a whole picture of what his life had actually been and to try to imagine how it must always have seemed to him" (159). Spurred by Holly's challenge, Phillip abandons the idea of forgetting for that of imaginatively re-creating. The results are far-reaching. "Instead of forgetting," Phillip writes, "I soon discovered that I was now able to imagine more about Father's life than I had in the past ever had any conception of—not of his professional life or his business affairs, though I felt I understood more of all that than I had previously realized, and not his family life even, but his inner life, his inmost, profoundest feelings about the world he was born into and in which he was destined to pass his youth and most of his adult years" (159).

Under what he at several places calls Holly's "spell," Phillip revises what he had once seen as his father's "willfulness, his selfishness, and even a certain ruthlessness" into "evidence of his imagination about himself and the kind of life he could make." Once Phillip's oppressor, Mr. Carver now becomes his hero, a man of energy and action, a man, Phillip writes, whom he "could admire without reservation, like a character in a book" (177).

Although Holly's advice at first glance seems entirely positive in its call for imaginative sympathy (underscored by Phillip's growth in this respect), on closer examination it appears flawed in its rigidity. Holly's ideas on sympathetic understanding, as Phillip eventually comes to see, have less to do with truthfully reimagining the past than with re-creating it entirely according to her own needs, as we can see in her reconstruction of her troubled relationship with her own father. As Phillip had done, Holly years earlier had bolted to New York to escape what she saw as the suffocating confines of family life; but now, feeling the emptiness of her present life, she finds herself envying the passion and caring that underpin the lives of her sisters and brothers who stayed in Cleveland and raised families. After a trip home for her mother's funeral, she begins to reassess her upbringing by re-creating her father into a paragon of virtue. Holly's reevaluation clearly has less to do with her father than her own needs; her making him into a hero signifies to her her growing beyond adolescent rebelliousness and, of more importance, reconnects her, in the only way now left to her, to her family. Phillip correctly observes that Holly's reconstructions are thoroughly willed, Holly "teaching herself to admire and respect her old patriarch of a father as she had not done since before her adolescence" (159). Phillip himself comes to see that his own reconstructions of his father are in all likelihood similarly self-serving. "It was mostly under Holly's influence that I came to a so much more interesting and enlightened view of him," Phillip writes. "If in the final analysis it was not an altogether accurate view, still it was at the time immensely gratifying to me" (162). Eventually, Holly's views about her own father harden into unreasonable generalizations about all fathers: she claims that not only did her father do no wrong in regard to his children, but that, more generally, all fathers, Phillip reports her saying, "were bound to be right in all disputations so far as their own children were concerned" (181). If Phillip is right that Jo and Betsy are frozen in roles of "injured adolescents" because they "could not forget the old injuries" (146), Holly is frozen in the role of dutiful and adoring child because she no longer will acknowledge the injuries inflicted by her father.

Holly's views on reconstructing the past, then, take their place at the opposite end of the spectrum from Phillip's on forgetting; both are unsatisfactory solutions to working through one's resentments because they deny the validity of one's deep feelings. Both are willed acts, the imposition of rigid narrative frames that distort in their inflexibility; in this, they stand in sharp contrast to the "endless remembering" of the cognitive artist who constantly reworks and remakes memories without freezing them into an unyielding totalized form. Both, finally, ignore the option of forgiveness because one's hurts are no longer recognized as significant. But it is precisely forgiveness that Taylor suggests leads to maturity. In the process of forgiving, one first acknowledges one's feelings of resentment and then, through imaginative sympathy, reworks that resentment into understanding. From understanding follows forgiveness, a celebratory joining of self and other. Forgiveness, then, might be best understood as the primary characteristic of the cognitive artist, the process of forgiving mirroring the creative recasting of memories for sympathetic insight and vision.

Certainly, it is Mr. Carver's forgiveness of Lewis Shackleford that allows for their joyous reunion, and their joyful friendship stands in dramatic contrast to the doings of his unforgiving—and unfulfilled—children. If Jo and Betsy learn nothing about reconciliation from the example of Mr. Carver and Mr. Shackleford, Phillip apparently does, inching toward a meaningful reunion with his father. Once back in New York, Phillip begins phoning his father, and their conversations quickly start knocking down the barriers that have divided them. "On the long-distance telephone we were able to speak of things we had never been able to talk about face to face," Phillip writes. "I can't say why this was so, not for certain. Often it would seem to me that it was not my father I was talking with but some other man who was very much like him. Or I would find myself visualizing him not as he looked now but as he looked when I was in my teens or even younger" (207). Phillip finds himself seized by an unaccustomed joy during his phone conversations.

But because Phillip never forgives his father, his reconciliation with him is incomplete, a state of affairs suggested by the very fact that their relationship blossoms only over the phone, when they sit a thousand miles apart. As we have seen in his earlier dealings with his father, Phillip's feelings toward him are typically reasonable and conciliatory when he is in New York thinking about life in Memphis; whenever he returns to Memphis, however, Phillip's deep-seated resentments toward his father usually surface to overwhelm his good-intentioned thoughts and plans. It is the great distance between them that allows Phillip and his father to talk freely on the phone of things they do not normally speak about when they are together, just as it is this distance that makes it seem for Phillip "that it was not my father I was talking with" (207). Over the phone Phillip moves toward a reconciliation with his father, but it is his father rewritten as someone else, a man who never betrayed his son, a man with whom Phillip has no quarrel. There is no forgiveness because there has been no hurt. Phillip's remaking of his father is the stuff of fantasy: he both forgets and idealizes, creating his father into the fictional character who best serves Phillip's needs, particularly his desire to deny the disturbing truth that he betrayed his father by failing to act on his behalf against Jo and Betsy.

The flimsiness, if not downright falsity, of Phillip's—and Holly's—reconciliations with their fathers is underscored in Phillip's matter-of-fact reporting of their deaths. Clearly, neither he nor Holly suffered much beyond the inconvenience of having to attend the last rites. "Of course each of us had to go to the funeral—Holly to Cleveland, I to Memphis," he writes (207). These trips home may be the last of their lives, or at least the last for some time, for both now retreat into the comfort and serenity of their quiet apartment life together—a life of passionless routine, free of intrusion from the present world ten stories below and the world of their pasts. "We have our serenity of course and we have put Memphis and Cleveland out of our lives," Phillip writes. "Those places mean nothing to us nowadays. And surely there is nothing in the world that can interfere with the peace and quiet of life in our tenth-floor apartment" (208).

Phillip's quiet acceptance of his remote and weightless life suggests how little he finally has learned from the narrative he has constructed. In exploring his memories and narrating his effort to create a meaningful story from them, Phillip no doubt has a richer understanding of himself and his father. And yet in the end he pulls back from the disturbing implications of this knowledge, reworking the story so as to justify rather than to interrogate and thus deepen his present life. Ironically, Phillip's narrative, particularly in its depiction of his father's drive and fortitude, everywhere offers him examples of evidence that calls into question his own serene life and suggests alternatives to it. But Phillip is a poor reader of his narrative and misses most of this; he is much better at using his own experiences to understand his father than he is at using his father's to understand himself.

Although Phillip focuses his narrative so overtly on his father, his narrative's true subject, judging from Phillip's final perspective on things, is his mother. Despite—or perhaps because of—the fact that she is mostly absent, her presence hovers ghostlike over and around the narrative, particularly at the end when Phillip envisions his future life with Holly, a bodiless existence with the two of them quietly fading away into nothingness. His future life will not be that of his father, a man of action who knew what he wanted and always took forceful action to get it, but of his mother, an emotional cripple who retreated from life to live out her days as an invalid in her room. Once again, Phillip misses all this. The absence of any meaningful commentary by Phillip on his mother's removal is the gap in his narrative that signifies what he refuses to see: that like his mother he is emotionally stunted, his serenity less a victory than a defeat, a giving in to the challenges of life, an escape into the torpor of life-sapping isolation and self-justification.

Finally, then, Phillip is anything but the cognitive artist that Taylor typically celebrates, despite the fact of his "endless remembering." In light of Phillip's situation, Taylor's comment that writing is an effort "to understand life, and you can only get the illusion of doing it fully by writing" (qtd. in Thompson 158) might best be understood as a warning that the writer can fall prey to the illusion of complete knowledge and make ill use of it. Rather than destabilizing the authoritarian self, Phillip's narrative only reinforces his belief in that self's superiority, suggested by his contentment in his isolation at the end and his comment that "there is nothing in the world that can interfere with the peace and quiet" (208) of his apartment world. Phillip finally is as sterile and weightless as the ghost of his mother; and appropriately, the only narrative he can imagine for himself and Holly is their fading away into thin air, not being "alive enough to have the strength to die." "Our serenity will merely have been translated into a serenity in another realm," he goes on. "How else, I ask myself, can one think of the end of two such serenely free spirits as Holly Kaplan and I?" (209). Phillip's denial of death here is also his denial of life and also the denial of the way of the cognitive artist who forever wrestles with matters of living and dying. Phillip's narrative ends with his un-answered question; typically, he fails to see the answer to it right before his eyes—the blank page.

Reminiscences

Recollections of Peter Taylor

CLEANTH BROOKS

It is impossible for me to say just when I first saw the name of Peter Taylor or read any of his stories. I do remember, however, the circumstances under which we got in touch with him when Robert Penn Warren and I were editing *The Southern Review*. It must have been in the late 1930s. Allen Tate, who I think had come in contact with Peter when he was teaching at Southwestern University in Memphis, wrote to us to tell us of this really remarkable young fiction writer and urged us to look carefully at any manuscripts that he might send us. We were indeed welcoming such material, and our welcome was the heartier when we saw Peter's first stories.

By this time, I don't believe he could have been more than his mid-twenties, if that far along. But the stories were brilliantly written, well-constructed, making use of materials that Peter apparently knew thoroughly, and finally excellently done. Naturally, we were happy to have them and did print them right along—several of them in the first series of *The Southern Review*.

Yet I am not positive that I had actually met Peter—perhaps I had, briefly—until he and his friend Robert Lowell and Jean Stafford, Robert Lowell's bride, came down from Ohio to the Louisiana State University in the very late 1930s.

John Crowe Ransom, the friend and former teacher of Red Warren and myself at Vanderbilt, sent me word that there was a very fine young couple at Kenyon who were now at loose ends. They were recently married. The young husband was a writer-to-be, clearly; and could we possibly have a post on *The Southern Review* which Jean Stafford, his wife, could occupy. If we did, this would allow the young couple to come to Baton Rouge and Robert to do another year's work—this time graduate work. The war was on. Everything was unsettled, but this would at least fill in not unusefully, he hoped, for a difficult period.

I know that Warren was out of town, and I believe he may have been in Italy at the time. At any rate, I let Ransom know at once that it had just happened we had lost our secretary and were very happy to have a chance of getting a new one. So down they came to take up their academic year's stay at Louisiana State University.

They came in, I remember, one evening after a long and exhausting train ride from somewhere in Ohio, and we had them, I suppose, for dinner, certainly for an evening at our little house in Baton Rouge.

The three of them showed the effects of their long journey. They were a little battle weary, indeed. In fact, I remember my wife writing to a friend of hers, declaring that Jean was certainly a "battered bride," by which she did not mean to disparage Jean's looks. Jean was a rather pretty young woman, but the general weariness that radiated from her, and the rest of them, was apparent.

It was a pleasant evening for us. We didn't keep them up too late. One event that does stick in my mind is this. We had at that time a little Boston terrier, a beautiful animal, right bred but with a disturbed mentality. He demanded being petted. He loved to be cuddled, but if you put your hands on him too rashly, he was likely to bite the blood out of them. Indeed, our little Boston terrier was what in a human being would be called insane. (Some time later on we found he was simply intolerable to live with and had him put to sleep.)

On this evening, however, he was very much about himself, very eager to find strangers in the house, and Robert Lowell was getting ready to cuddle him when we warned him off, and Peter Taylor, I remember, said, "Yes, we must keep these two highly bred young Bostonians from getting too much into the way of each other." It was indeed an accurate comment, done in good humor, and fitting the situation exactly. No one could doubt Robert Lowell's being a highbred Bostonian and so — in his own strange little field — so was our puppy dog.

I had Robert Lowell and Peter Taylor in my classes that year, graduate classes they were, and they were brilliant students. Robert Penn Warren had them, of course, in his classes too and made the same report.

But it was plain that neither of these young men was going to become college professors. Their papers were brilliant. They wrote beautifully, for they were writers-to-be and were already writing excellent English prose, but their fate was plainly different to our eyes.

I must confess that I did not realize Jean Stafford's literary ambitions until a good deal later. It was a long time before I discovered that she had been going back after hours to the office and whacking away at her first novel, a successful one, called *Boston Adventure*. We didn't get to know Jean very well this first year, but we did get to know her better in the years that followed, and she and my wife, in particular, had a fondness for each other. We saw Jean from time to time after she had come back north and we had come to Yale. She visited us on several occasions.

What has all of this to do with Peter Taylor? Not very much directly, but my memory was never very good and is getting worse, I regret to say. We did see a good deal of Robert Lowell and Peter Taylor during that academic year, but they ran with a somewhat younger crowd, and the year was an intensely busy one, not only for them but for Warren and me. At any rate, though I remember many pleasant meetings, nothing particular sticks out except Peter's sweet, calm disposition and his neat wit and his quiet, charming demeanor.

Then the Second World War came about; the Lowells went north, and Peter got into the army fairly quickly and was working with it in Tennessee. I remember my wife and I were driving up from Baton Rouge to New York and taking Jean Stafford with us to drop her off at Chattanooga for an appointment to see a person who had become her good friend, Peter Taylor. He was always a good friend of Jean's and of Robert's—even after their separation.

In the later years we did not see much of Peter. The few times were precious ones. We kept up a friendship, and I saw him not only in Tennessee but in New York and later on in North Carolina, where Peter had already bought one of his several houses. He loved old houses and had a good taste for them and before things were over with had bought and used a number. This was a trait that he shared with my wife, for later on in Connecticut, after I had come to Yale, she bought for us or at least superintended the buying of a Connecticut saltbox house of 1720 vintage, and we got it moved three miles and erected it on the perfect site. We had nearly thirty years of happiness there.

So we did see Peter from time to time at various places and, of course, kept up with his brilliant career. I not only knew his stories as they came out but also enjoyed very much a volume of short plays that he did, plays that revealed a talent that I did not know he possessed. They were very good. I don't know whether any of them were produced widely or not.

My last meeting with Peter occurred about four or five years ago when we found ourselves on the same platform in Nashville, Tennessee, at some literary event. It was nice even in those constricted and baffling quarters to have a chance to chat a little with each other, and I remember Peter's reading a very interesting excerpt from a novel. Yet, was this the very last time we met? I'm not sure. I do remember another event, however. I was talking to Peter about his Pulitzer Prize novel titled *A Summons to Memphis*. It is a rather nice piece of work, and shows Peter at his best in his latest work, which I would regard as a kind of delightful social comedy. Part of this story—in fact, a good part of the story—has to do with the difference between the quality of life in Nashville and the quality of life in Memphis. A family moves from Nashville to Memphis, and we find that they encounter a whole number of differences. A typical one is in some matters of pronunciation. I remember, since I have some connection with both cities, that in Nashville, when Greta Garbo's picture, I forget the title but one of her big early successes, came out, we were told that

Nashville was shown the artistic, the sad, ending, whereas they gave Memphis the happy, commonplace ending. I'm not saying this to disparage Memphis, then or now. I'm simply telling a story. But the Nashville folk were very happy at the distinction and thought it quite relevant. When I told the story to Peter, he said, "I wish you'd let me know this event in time. It makes the point nicely, the point I was making in my novel. I certainly should have used it."

Peter Taylor
and the Kenyon Connection

DAVID H. LYNN

> They reached the dark quarters; they could see lights still burning in Mr.
> Hubert's house and somebody was blowing the fox-horn again and it wasn't
> any boy and he had never heard a fox-horn sound mad before either, and he
> and Uncle Buck scattered out on the slope below Tennie's cabin.

NOT PETER TAYLOR—William Faulkner, from his story "Was." Early in the autumn of 1977, however, Peter Taylor devoted the greater part of a graduate workshop to reading this story aloud himself. A chancy pedagogy. Not many writing teachers—not many successful ones—would do such a thing, waste a precious hour.

Now I had read this story before. I'd read most of Faulkner's fiction as an undergraduate at Kenyon College. I could speak with reason about his thematic webs of time passing and past and timelessness, of balked generations, of the kudzu-like Snopseses. And on that autumn day in Peter Taylor's workshop, as Miss Sophonsiba trapped Uncle Buck and lost him again to Uncle Buddy, I discovered that I'd been deaf as a stone to Faulkner's language. I'd mistaken this as the same language we spoke in Michigan and Ohio, rather than a different tongue entirely.

How that sentence spins on: " . . . and somebody was blowing the fox-horn again and it wasn't any boy and he had never heard a fox-horn sound mad before either." Peter Taylor paid it out slowly, a rope that demanded careful handling. His long, loping, mellifluous Tennessee cadence allowed Faulkner's Mississippian phrases to slip into place gently and inevitably. What had been a Jamesian gray mass of words on the page seemed suddenly right and light and even rather simple. For the first time I glimpsed Faulkner the Southern Chronicler, the teller of tales, the keeper of memories. I learned, too, how to hear Taylor's own stories, many of which I'd read before but had never heard aloud, had never *heard* at all.

More. In this lesson, Taylor was teaching us about voice, about rhythm and pattern, certainly about humor. About pace. He was teaching younger writers how to read and hear as writers.

If I'd studied Faulkner at Kenyon in the early 1970s, that's also where I discovered Peter Taylor's work because he too had been an undergraduate in

Gambier. His is a special place in the pantheon of legendary writers who jour-
neyed to the wilds of central Ohio in the 1940s and 50s to work with John
Crowe Ransom. It would have been enough that the roommate who became
his lifelong friend was Robert Lowell and that Taylor's own star would rise
steadily over the next thirty years. But two of his finest stories, "1939" and
"Dean of Men," also directly involve Kenyon. And Taylor returned to Gambier
in the 1950s as a teacher and heir apparent to Ransom as editor of *The Kenyon
Review.*

Influenced perhaps by Lowell's growing concern in the 1950s with autobiography as a subject as well as source of art, Taylor's story "1939" draws directly on their experiences as Ransom's students in Gambier. In it he makes a
point about how the young writers saw themselves as set apart: "Generally
speaking, we at Douglass House [a separate house in the center of the village]
were reviled by the rest of the student body, all of whom lived in the vine-
covered dormitories facing the campus" (*CS* 329).

Once discovered, "1939" became a lens through which to view the college. While I was a freshman, my Resident Assistant, an honors English major,
would slip away for private chats about poetry with John Crowe Ransom.
Ransom was long retired, a legend sometimes glimpsed but no longer demon-
strably involved with the college. *The Kenyon Review* itself was moribund,
having passed through a series of editors after Ransom.

For students of my era interested in writing fiction and poetry, those heady
times described in "1939" seemed distant indeed. Although the college remained remote, traditional, and largely privileged, Vietnam and Watergate had
thrust us into a different world entirely. And we ourselves lacked even the clear
demarcations of a Douglass House by which to define ourselves as writers, or
at least as apprentices to the craft. By the time I graduated I knew that, after
a year writing on my own, I would apply to the University of Virginia to work
with Peter Taylor. Consciously or not, I would be making contact with those
vanished forebears.

I was with Peter Taylor the day Robert Lowell died. No, I've believed that
for fifteen years, and now that I check the dates, I realize it isn't true, that I
sat in Peter Taylor's workshop the day *after* Lowell died, though Taylor would
only have learned the news late the night before. And this isn't the only surprise: Lowell died on September 12, 1977. I'd have sworn it was later that fall,
that I'd already established a friendship with Peter Taylor myself, not that I'd
been in Charlottesville for only a couple of weeks. Yet the core of the memory
remains vivid. Taylor arrives for the workshop as usual. His plane for Boston won't leave until later in the day, and this is a way to keep occupied. (Do
we already know? Has the word passed among us? Are we certain he will
show?) As always he wears a comfortable jacket and tie, but he looks drawn,
shaken, somewhat distracted. He fumbles a broken-backed old briefcase onto

the table. Vivid, but I don't remember how he begins, whether he announces his loss or assumes we know. From the satchel he draws a jumbled handful of letters. "These are thirty-some years' worth of letters from Cal," he says. "I've been looking through them, for bits and pieces to read in Boston. I thought perhaps you might be interested, as writers, in what he has to say about writing."

For the next hour or so he leafs through the papers for passages to read aloud, hunting for ones he's recalled, allowing himself to be waylaid by others, halting halfway through memories that become too personal or "can't interest anyone" any longer. His voice is soft as he reads. He fills in gaps. Explains where necessary. His tone shifts from the affectionate to the puzzled to the businesslike. In back, behind words and tone, I sense distantly something of what he would later tell Lowell's biographer, Ian Hamilton: that he " 'felt angry with Cal,' as if Lowell had voluntarily elected to walk out on his old friend" (475). But I am also aware that he's already shaping a story. He's making sense of Lowell's death by telling us a tale.

To enter the writing program at the University of Virginia in the late 1970s was to enter into a conversation with Peter Taylor. That conversation was never merely limited to two or to a workshop or even to an immediate room, however. It seemed never to hush but to be always in the air, manifesting itself usually in stories Peter would be recounting about family, about friends, comparing scandals large and small. A young writer would observe and listen, be caught up in the wash of story and language, might test the water with a tidbit of one's own.

And this was very much how Taylor led his workshops as well. They too were conversations. Here we engaged writers living and dead: Flaubert, Chekhov, and James; Welty, Warren, and Porter; our own efforts; a conversation; a give-and-take.

A principal lesson for many of us, separate from any direct aspect of pen on paper, had to do with Taylor's belief in a balance to one's life, about the utter seriousness with which he protected the time and energy he would need for his writing. On the one hand, he was a presence in the English department and in the town. He loved cocktail parties that offered plenty to watch and listen to and, with any luck, be shocked by. Off to one side he'd be circled by friends listening to one story or another, his silver pocket flask safely tucked in his jacket pocket. And he enjoyed the formal croquet matches played by elderly members of Charlottesville's horsy set—they'd joust with the same ruthlessness as the Ransoms in Gambier.

On the other hand, we came to see that what came first, came before everything, was his morning's work. Slow, steady, pencil and paper. These were potent years for Peter Taylor, a second spring for his own work. After a relatively fallow period, after a major heart attack, *In the Miro District and Other*

Stories appeared in 1976, containing some of Taylor's greatest work, of a depth
and subtlety beyond his earlier stories. Soon *The Old Forest and Other Stories*
would follow. And, eventually, in 1986, came the novel *A Summons to Memphis,* which brought him wider fame and award.

It was Peter Taylor who persuaded me to continue for a doctorate—arguing for the importance of a career separate from one's writing. By chance
rather than design, I eventually returned to Kenyon.

By John Crowe Ransom's design rather than by chance, Peter Taylor had
returned to Kenyon in 1952 as a member of the English department. Ransom
enlisted him as an advisory editor of the *Review.* Taylor has claimed that the
position was largely honorary—that Ransom rarely consulted him. "He remembered having read only a dozen stories or so during the five years he lived
in Gambier" (Janssen 272). But Ransom privately intended that Peter Taylor
should be his successor as editor.

Taylor's initial response to the plan was enthusiastic. A letter he wrote
to Randall Jarrell in March 1957 is wonderfully revealing of his character,
both self-deprecating and full of his sense of the challenge. "Please don't laugh.
... Mr. Ransom and everyone else concerned has urged me to take it over and
... to make a different sort of magazine of it—which means one devoted almost entirely to fiction and poetry and plays. ... I really tried to get out of
doing this. ... But their pressure and my own vanity and ugly ambition and
the thought that a lot of it would be really fun decided me finally to do it"
(Janssen 273).

But Taylor soon decided against taking up the editorship. This choice
turned, as at other crucial moments in his career, on his sense of protecting his
personal resources. To take up the burdens of editing would be, at the very
least, to deflect him from his own stories and plays.

Another motive may have been his fury at the acting president of the college, Frank Bailey. Faculty homes in those days were assigned according to
seniority. But Bailey, perhaps acting on a grudge, intervened to prevent Taylor
from moving to a fine brick house that, according to precedent, should have
been his. Houses have always been a passion for the Taylors, and he resigned
his post and left Gambier the following year. My guess, however, is that he felt
it was time, given his decision about the *Review,* to move on in any event. He
also adapted the incident with President Bailey into the central event in "Dean
of Men," his second story set largely at Kenyon. Revenge and inspiration may
stroll hand in hand.

Four months after Robert Lowell, my father died unexpectedly. The phone
call from my sister woke me in the grayish predawn January light. The flight I
booked to Detroit would not leave until late afternoon. Why should I cancel a
lunch date with Peter Taylor, any more than he had canceled class earlier in the
year? Sitting alone would hardly be preferable.

Peter picked me up at Wilson Hall (he'd invited me to share his office with the two large windows in what was otherwise a mausoleum), and we drove to a small place for a sandwich. One difference: I couldn't assume he'd heard my news, nor was I able to tell him over the table. What did we talk about? It must have been the usual—what we were reading, how our work was going, some gossip certainly, ideas for or stories about interesting travel.

After lunch we drove back to the university. He pulled into the small parking lot behind Wilson Hall. And there, as I was about to get out of the car, I finally mentioned that I'd be missing the next workshop or two, and why. Peter nodded and turned the car off. It was very quiet. And then he was telling me about his own father's death, about the awkwardness, the tensions in the family. He sat turned in the driver's seat, arm on the back, his hat bumping against the roof. He was telling me a tale, sharing one, making sense of what we'd both experienced and of the world.

The Dancer and the Dance

ROBERT WILSON

WHEN I FIRST got to know Peter Taylor, in the fall of 1975, I had read only a handful of his stories, and those few I'd read passively, with the undergraduate's sleepy acceptance that what I was reading was important because a teacher had told me so. In this case it was two teachers, James Boatwright and Stephen Goodwin. Steve also told me that, if I wanted to write, as I did, I should go to Charlottesville and affix myself to Peter. So I got accepted to the graduate English program at Virginia, quit the job I'd had since graduating from college, and moved with my wife, Martha, to an ugly complex of "garden" apartments on the outskirts of Charlottesville. The first day Peter kept office hours at the university I showed up at his door. When he opened it, I said, "Steve Goodwin and Jim Boatwright sent me to study with you," and he said, without a moment's hesitation—well, I can't quite remember what he said. I tend to think of him as throwing his arms wide open and even giving me a hug, but that isn't Peter's style at all, so whatever he said must have been the verbal equivalent of that. What I do remember is that, within the week, Martha and I had been invited to Peter's house, that Peter had murmured something about a teaching job he might be able to get for me in Greensboro, and that the friendship that has been among the most important in my life was well under way. This was, perhaps fortunately, before he had read a word of my prose.

Before long, I began to apply myself to his prose, reading it, if only because I was beginning to read the man as well, as I had never read fiction before. I was living in it. There's a story about Eudora Welty that Peter's wife, Eleanor, likes to tell, about Miss Welty's receiving a call from the Friends of the Library in some nearby Mississippi town. The voice on the line said, "Miss Eudora, we'd like you to come over to the library and tell us some of your stories in your own words." I would read a story of Peter's, when I was supposed to be reading Milton or Yeats or somebody insignificant like that, and then I'd go to Peter's office the next day and say, "I read 'Je Suis Perdu' last night," and then he would tell the story again—in his own words.

I went through most of his published work that way, and then I also heard him talking about stories he was working on. It was the spring of 1976, I think, when his great story "In the Miro District" appeared in *The New Yorker,* and just before that Peter and another student and I drove from Charlottesville to Norwood, North Carolina, to pick up furniture that Peter was moving among his several houses. I made at least one other long trip with Peter moving furniture, this one in a huge rental truck, and on both trips Peter offered as payment just what I most wanted, a full measure of himself. The talk never stopped, not even at meals, when I would be sitting with plate cleaned, and Peter, who is not what you'd call uninterested in food, would discover that he'd barely touched his meal and gulp it down while I managed a few sentences of my own history or observations. But the point is that on the first furniture-moving trip he talked at length about "In the Miro District," not stinting on Tennessee history or a hundred other things, so that when I would come to read and reread that extraordinarily complex and layered story it would seem almost like an outline of all that was in his mind.

I remember reading "The Old Forest" in long galley sheets from *The New Yorker.* It was the middle of the night in a room at the Pier House in Key West. Martha and I—and Steve Goodwin and his girlfriend at the time—were visiting down there, where Peter and Eleanor had a house. I took the galleys back to Peter early the next morning, wondering what I could possibly say about such an extraordinary story—and was treated to a long, detailed monologue about the Memphis "demimonde."

Years later, when *A Summons to Memphis* was published, I decided to review it for the newspaper where I work. A friend was also writing about it for her publication, *The New Republic,* and the two of us had a long lunch at a Chinese restaurant and puzzled over the novel for a good two hours, feeling finally as if we'd barely scratched the surface. Near the end of the lunch, after my friend and I had circled round and round that quite circular story, we stared with something like disbelief at each other, and one of us—I can't remember which, because the same thought occurred to both of us in almost the same language—said, "My God, he's tearing it all down—everything." As it happens, Peter and Eleanor were living in Georgetown at the time, across the river from my office, and I would walk over the bridge and have lunch with him. That week I tested out some of our theories about the book on him, and I remember his laughing and saying, "Oh, it's all there in the last paragraph." I remember, too, that Peter and I talked about the quote from Hardy at the end of the novel. Somehow, neither of us could recall which poem it was from, although we both know the poem, "Neutral Tones," which is a fairly famous one.

Part of what I'm trying to say, I guess, is that I am hopelessly compromised as a critic of Peter's work. I've never been able to separate the dancer from the dance. I love and admire both Peter and his writing, and although I've spent sixteen years trying to puzzle out both of them, I'm still largely mystified by them.

As a writer, or, as I think I am obliged to say, as a would-be writer, I've of course tried to learn from Peter's work, as I have from all the writers I most admire. More and more, though, I think that writers of real genius teach you only how inimitable they are and how useful genius is. I can't imagine learning anything much about how to write from D. H. Lawrence, for instance. It would be ludicrous to try to write like him. Beyond this, I've felt sometimes that knowing Peter and his work so well is a little like flying too close to the sun. All great writers seem to switch metaphors, to create a vortex. Think of the writers still being swallowed up by the genius of Faulkner. I don't believe that anyone ever has or ever will accuse me of writing like Peter, but his work has in some sense paralyzed me, and I've seen this happen to other students of his as well. The layers in his stories. The ambition of them. The confidence behind that shambling narrative voice. What rational person could hope to write like that?

And Peter is so unnervingly lofty about what he himself reads. It's always Chekhov or Tolstoy or Lawrence or James. He does not bother with his contemporaries, or only rarely does. This is not so much out of a sense of his own superiority, I think, as a feeling that there is too little time for anything but the best. It's true, too, that much of what he reads he reads aloud to Eleanor, or it is read to him by her, and there are very few of his contemporaries who can hold up to being read out loud.

Of course Peter does not mean to intimidate. As a teacher and a friend he is all encouragement. He seems genuinely pleased each time I tell him I'm working on something new, and I know that I can send him anything I do finish, and he will read it with care and generosity. Still, it is difficult not to want to emulate his high standards. Once, after I'd finished a novel, I told him with a foolish haughtiness that I would send it to only a few publishers, because if it were a good book it would be recognized as such immediately and I didn't see the point of publishing a mediocre one. "Oh, go ahead and publish it if you can," he said, without a trace of anything but sincere goodwill and friendship. "There's nothing wrong with publishing a mediocre book. Having it in print will encourage you to write the next one."

Two Audiences for "Emmagene"

MADISON SMARTT BELL

I HAVE HAD the interesting and pleasant experience of hearing Peter Taylor read one of my favorite of his stories on two separate occasions, before two very different audiences, and ten years apart. The first time was part of a joint appearance with Robert Lowell at Vanderbilt University, around the time of the publication of *In the Miro District*. The second time was a solo appearance by Mr. Taylor at the Donnell Library in New York City. The story was "The Hand of Emmagene."

The Vanderbilt audience was the older of the two, in my estimation. I would have called the average age of those in attendance somewhere between forty and fifty. These were, I think, for the most part consumers or in some cases teachers and critics of literature. Not so many practitioners or would-be practitioners among them (saving myself—a very minor threat at age seventeen). In the New York audience, which was among other things considerably smaller, the average age was closer to thirty, I would guess. Add on the ten years intervening and you are really beginning to talk about a different generation. This was not just a group of readers and scholars, but an audience of beginning and aspiring writers, students and recent alumni of the various graduate creative writing programs around town, and so on.

"The Hand of Emmagene" is one of Mr. Taylor's verse stories—the best of them if you ask me. Most of you probably know it well enough, but in case it's been a while, I will review a few salient points. It is one of Mr. Taylor's shorter stories, especially if you consider that the lines don't go all the way to the edge of the page, but also one of the most complicated. In spite of its brevity it has a quite deep historical background and its narrative strategy is, shall we say, multidimensional.

The story is told by one of Mr. Taylor's more disingenuous first-person narrators. It's difficult to tell from the first at least whether he is distorting things on purpose or if he is a successful self-deceiver. Perhaps these options are not mutually exclusive. Anyway, this gentleman is a member of the Nashville upper crust. He lives alone with his wife, and they have a long-standing habit of importing distant cousins from the country community of their origin to use as companions, more or less, for a couple of years until they marry and go back home. Despite a considerable amount of lip service paid by this narrator to the importance of the kinship, there is a class barrier between himself and these country cousins that is, in his mind at least, completely impermeable. This is where the trouble starts, although it is by no means the end of it.

The actions and speech of Emmagene provide the story with a second voice. She turns out to be a rather dour young woman with a strong religious streak, who prefers work to leisure, takes over most of the housekeeping tasks from the professional servants, and would rather sit home with her Bible than go out on dates once her maid's work is done. This isn't too much of a problem until a year or so goes by and it becomes evident to the narrator that Emmagene has no intention of returning to the country, married or not. She would rather stay in town, go to school, perhaps meet and marry an upper-class Nashville boy. At this point the careful listener will have understood that the narrator is the sort of man who believes there is nothing worse than social inappropriateness. The rest of the story is about how he learns otherwise.

For the narrator, Emmagene has become a problem that has to be solved. His solution is to tactfully, subtly, and absolutely compel her to accept the attentions of the country boys who have begun to cruise the house in their jacked-up cars. It is a near imperceptible but inexorable piece of manipulation. Emmagene starts to go out with the boys, and the narrator and his wife breathe a sigh of relief, believing that marriage and departure will shortly ensue. They make themselves smoothly and suavely deaf to Emmagene's elliptical complaints to the effect that the boys are not particularly nice, that in her relations with them she is forced to do things that are spiritually repugnant to her. There is something especially offensive that she is obliged to do with one of her hands, which her hosts especially don't want to hear about.

The Nashville audience listened to the reading of this story very quietly and seriously right from the beginning. These listeners seemed to pick up very quickly that this narrator was not to be trusted. There is a kind of moral queasiness in the very sound of his voice. Nevertheless, it is possible to see the events and the characters through the tint the narrator wants to give them. One sees that Emmagene is a dismayingly strong person, that the narrator is afraid of her strength. One begins to realize that the narrator's set of manipulative devices are unlikely to be adequate for the management of a person like Emmagene. Big trouble is on the way sure enough. Among the Nashville listeners (who were hearing the story prior to its publication) the mood was apprehensive. Dreadful, you might say.

With the New York crowd things were very different. They seemed to receive the story one-dimensionally. They seemed to take the narrator entirely at his word, indeed, to identify with him completely. To his wriggles and knowing asides they added their own sniggers and smirks. They saw Emmagene as a comical figure, a cartoon hick. They participated fully in the narrator's fatal underestimation of her.

From where I slumped in my seat it appeared to me that Mr. Taylor noticed this reaction and began to play upon it. He began deliberately to play the story for laughs, it seemed. And it played very well that way. The New Yorkers found the sexual innuendo especially amusing. For me, there was a certain sadistic pleasure, though, in knowing where it was all headed. Emmagene is not the sort of person it is safe to ignore. When she finds that she can communicate her problem in no other way, she resorts to demonstration, using her left hand, and a hatchet. The story becomes a gruesome elaboration of the Biblical recommendation: "If thy right hand offend thee, cut it off and cast it from thee." If nothing else, it goes to show that spiritual edicts are quite real for some people.

Imagine the effect of this ending on people who had no idea it was coming. It was the most successful sucker punch I have ever been witness to. A moan went through the Donnell Library as if everyone there had suddenly been hit in the belly with a big load of grapeshot. You never saw a sicker looking bunch of sophisticates in your life.

Still, after my initial wave of glee had passed over, the whole experience was a little depressing. The New York audience was very much an audience of writers, remember. They were more or less my peers, and some of them were my friends too, however much I enjoyed their discomfiture. Neither they nor I was capable of writing such a story, with its complex doubling of a deep history that tries to force itself up into the present, of a buried story that forces its way up through the surface of the story that is apparently being told. I couldn't write such a story today; I don't have the skills for it. That's not so bad. There is still time to learn. But it helps to know what there is to be learned. It worried me a little then, and it worries me a little now, that out of this group, a reasonably representative slice of the literati of my generation, or thereabouts, it was not only unlikely that anyone could have written such a story, but none of them even seemed to know that they should want to, and in fact, they didn't even know how to read it.

Interview

An Oracle of Mystery

A Conversation with Peter Taylor

THE FOLLOWING CONVERSATION took place between Peter Taylor and Christopher Metress in Sewanee, Tennessee, on the afternoon of 11 August 1993.

CM: It seems only appropriate that as I sit here this afternoon in Sewanee, on The Domain of the University of the South, talking to a "Southern writer," that I should begin with a question about place. So I'll ask you to recall the first time you ever came to Sewanee.

PT: I'd been coming to this part of Tennessee for years, over to Monteagle, before I ever came to Sewanee. My first visit to Sewanee wasn't until my college years when I came to stay with Robert Daniel, whose grandfather was the Episcopal Bishop of Tennessee. He lived in a big house not far from here with his Aunt Charlotte, who was a spinster. Robert and I were exploring life back then [he laughs], and one of the nice things about his aunt's old house—which is now the university president's house—was that there was an outdoor stairway that allowed us to get in and out at night without his Aunt Charlotte knowing. Back then, there wasn't a whole lot of trouble we could get into, and we didn't. But we enjoyed the freedom of coming and going as we pleased.

CM: And you've been coming back to Sewanee for the Writer's Conference for how many years now?

PT: About three years, maybe four, for the Writer's Conference. But I've been coming back to Sewanee, for one reason or another, since those days when I came to visit Robert Daniel. For many of those years I spent the summers over in Monteagle. But this year, Eleanor and I have purchased a house here in Sewanee. In fact, the house we just purchased we used to own, oh maybe ten years ago. We just recently purchased it again because we felt that we could work better here than in Monteagle.

Still, I love coming up here for the summer, and it's a great plus to have the Writer's Conference available. You get to meet so many interesting people, especially young writers whose work I might have altogether missed. And, of course, my good friend Andrew Lytle is just down the road in Monteagle, and has been there all his life. He's ninety now and full of life still. He's so remarkable. And you know, he lives in a log house his grandfather built—it's a fascinating house, full of interesting hallways and rooms—and I go to visit him as often as I can. Of course, long gone are the days when Allen Tate used to be here—he was another remarkable man. It used to be great fun to get Lytle and Tate together. The arguments they would have sometimes! Both such remarkable men. Which reminds me, this year at the conference a gentleman took a group of writers and students up to the local cemetery at midnight and read aloud "Ode to the Confederate Dead." Some of the local folks were a bit offended by all this, the candles, the full moon, the poetry. But Allen, oh he would have loved it. He lived for moments like that. It appealed to his sense of drama.

CM: One of your most recent stories, "The Witch of Owl Mountain Springs," focuses a great deal on this part of the country. In fact, at the beginning of the story, your narrator makes an interesting observation about the kind of world that existed here in the 1930s. He says, "Perhaps a realistic presentation of the place can best be stated negatively. No one imagined that Owl Mountain Springs itself was exactly a fashionable summer place, not even vaguely so—not in the eyes of the great world, at any rate. And yet it was as much respected for what it was *not* as for what it *was*" (OSC 119-20).

PT: People would come here from Memphis and Nashville and Chattanooga, from Louisville and Birmingham and even sometimes Atlanta. They were all so different and yet so very much alike. They were from very different parts of the region, from very different parts of Tennessee even, and yet they felt they all shared something. And I guess in many ways what they shared was not only a sense of who they were and what their world meant, but also who they weren't and what their world wasn't. Distinctions were so important. It was a fascinating place back then, full of people from a world that was slipping away. Despite this, maybe because of this, they would all still come here, perhaps as a way of defining themselves, I don't know. Whatever was going on, it fascinated me then and it obviously still fascinates me now. I'm still writing about it after all these years.

CM: Your most recent collection, *The Oracle at Stoneleigh Court,* was released in February . . .

PT: First of all, before we begin to discuss the collection, I want to thank you for helping me with three of the stories included in it. I want to make sure you put this into the interview, and so I better mention it before I forget, again. As you know, I wrote "In the Waiting Room," "The Real Ghost," and "At the Art Theatre" years ago and forgot about them. When you found the three manuscripts among my papers at Vanderbilt and sent them to me I was quite pleased. I reworked the stories, of course, but I was surprised by the quality of the original works, and I knew immediately that I wanted them in the collection. I meant to thank you, to acknowledge you somehow at the beginning of the collection, but to tell you the truth, I forgot. Eleanor, who always remembers everything I forget, reminded me of this after the book was already published, so I'd like now to acknowledge your help.

And another thing, those three stories have been praised very much more than I expected. I get more comments about "In the Waiting Room," "The Real Ghost," and "At the Art Theatre" than any of the other stories in *Oracle*. Of course, "The Real Ghost" and "At the Art Theatre" are the two shortest stories in the collection, so maybe that's all anybody is reading [he laughs]. I'd like to think not, but perhaps it's true. But I will say that I also hear a good deal about "The Decline and Fall of the Episcopal Church." [He pauses.] But, come to think of it, that's one of the shorter stories also. Oh, well.

CM: "The Decline and Fall of the Episcopal Church" is also a story you wrote many years ago. It was published back in the midseventies, wasn't it?

PT: Yes, that's right. I don't remember the exact year, but it was published in *The Sewanee Review* under the title, "Tom, Tell Him."

CM: I believe that Jay Tolson, in *USA Today*, said that "The Decline and Fall of the Episcopal Church" was the finest story in the collection.

PT: "Decline and Fall" was just buried—I don't know anyone who had ever read it. Andrew Lytle printed it in *The Sewanee Review*, which meant the story had some merit, but I never heard from anyone about it. But when I reread it a while ago, I liked it and wanted to get a wider audience for it. As I was putting this collection together I reread most of my uncollected fiction. I came across one story about the "Bell Witch" appearing in a Nashville streetcar ["Nerves"]. I originally published that one in *The New Yorker*, but nobody ever commented on it. I wanted a wider audience for that story as well, so I included it in the collection. There was still another story I wanted to reprint, but I can't remember the title right now.

I still have a half-dozen uncollected stories—but I remember one that I reread that I definitely didn't want to reprint. It's entitled "Uncles," and it appeared in *The New Yorker*. The reason I didn't reprint it, and never will, is because of the way it was written. You see, back then, I had a contract with *The New Yorker*. If you published four stories a year in *The New Yorker* they would pay you even more money for a fifth one. And *The New Yorker* paid very well in those days. One year, I had written four stories for them. Toward the end of that year they sent me a note saying that if I could write another story for them that they would pay me even more money. I remember I was in Greensboro at the time. Well, I immediately made up my mind to write that story. It took me about a week to write it. You see, I knew the kind of story they wanted. They took it, and I got that money, but I was sort of ashamed of it because I knew that *The New Yorker* liked stories about families and about specific places. So I put a lot of details about a specific place—I set the story in St. Louis—and wrote a story about family conflict.

CM: Did you consider reprinting it in your recent collection?

PT: I guess I did, but it wasn't a serious consideration. The story's not very good. Nor does it really fit into the "ghostly" elements of *Oracle*.

CM: There's one more early story in *Oracle* that we've yet to discuss, and that's "Demons." I remember the first time I read that story it didn't make the same impression on me as your more accomplished pieces, and yet when I was reading the new collection I was struck by the fact that not only does "Demons" fit in well with the collection's "ghostly" elements, but that it also stands on its own as a very fine story.

PT: I'm glad to hear that. That story has also received some praise, especially from more serious readers. I really enjoyed writing that story.

CM: There's a line in that story that seems to summarize one of the major themes of your present collection. Toward the end of the story the narrator says, "But still, how am I to explain the voices I heard as a child? . . . The truth is, I have come to like having them there at my beginning, unexplained, a mystery. My liking for the mystery of them has increased with every bit of learning I have had to do. Such a mystery becomes, finally, a kind of knowledge" (116).

PT: Well, you're right there. It's the mystery of things that I am trying to get at in *Oracle*.

CM: And so you've been pleased by the reception of the volume as whole?

PT: Oh yes. But the collection has not had altogether favorable reviews. For instance, the English reviews have not been as positive as the reviews here at home. And perhaps that's because there's a difference in the English sense of humor and drama. I don't know. Also, I think that in writing this volume I did take a change of direction, a change of purpose, focusing more on the mysterious than I had before.

CM: So perhaps the change in direction has disturbed some readers?

PT: Absolutely. Readers often don't like it when you change. If you do something well, they want you to keep on doing it that way.

CM: But while these stories do mark a change in direction—I think one critic said something to the effect that Peter Taylor has gone Southern Gothic—there are some definite continuities here with your earlier work. These ghost stories, these stories of mystery, do seem to be an extension of your earliest preoccupations.

PT: And yet there's a change too. You get to a time in your life when you become aware of differences, when you not only see things differently but are keenly aware that you do. And that is what I was trying to explore, my awareness of differences, especially my awareness it's so very difficult to understand things. My knowledge of mystery, if you will.

CM: And yet the very title of the collection, *The Oracle at Stoneleigh Court*, suggests knowledge, a way of knowing. We go to oracles, don't we, not only because we want to know things but also because we expect to get some answers?

PT: But do we get those answers?

CM: But that's what I wanted to ask you. In the beginning of the title story the narrator says his story "all seems significant or even ominous in some way that is quite beyond my understanding" (12). And then toward the very end, just after he has been married and all of the strange events are about to occur—Lila is about to have her accident at the very moment Aunt Gussie dies in the hospital—the narrator says, "And from this point forward in this narrative I will not be held responsible for explanation or interpretation of events that follow with seeming mystery one upon the another" (83).

PT: I wanted there to be at the end of the story a sort of captivation—not so much an understanding of events, but a fascination about what has occurred.

CM: So again, if there is an understanding achieved, it is an understanding of mystery, not certainty.

PT: Yes.

CM: This brings me to another point, then. So much of the title story is about storytelling. In Southern literature, storytelling is revered, and this reverence probably comes from many sources. But it seems to me that storytelling is so important to the Southern experience because storytelling, the oral tradition, has always served as a means of understanding history and community, of grasping some lost or hidden truth. You get this sense of recuperative storytelling in "The Oracle" when the narrator and Aunt Gussie first meet. She is able to tell him things about his past and himself that allow him to conjure up in his mind imagined scenes from his family history—his grandfather "in the guise of a young man lecturing in the Chautauqua series of the 1880s" or his grandfather "as the occupant of the Tennessee gubernatorial chair," for instance (35). At this point you suspect, or at least I suspect, that the narrator will slowly begin, through Aunt Gussie and her stories, to gain a deeper understanding of himself and the world around him—that in this story, storytelling will act as a means for achieving understanding. And yet, when we learn that the narrator has forgotten his heroic war experiences, that he has a "blank" spot in his past, the stories that others tell him so that he might recover that lost past—these stories not only frustrate him, but seem to impede his progress toward understanding himself and those events.

PT: Of course, part of that memory lapse is genuine—he is suffering from shell shock, but there is also a sense of purposefulness in his forgetting. He doesn't want to remember. So the stories he hears, he doesn't want to hear. It's not that they are getting in the way of his understanding. They may, in fact, be giving him too much understanding about himself, an understanding he doesn't want.

CM: So, despite his repeated declarations that he can't make sense of the past, what we have here is a narrator who may not want to make sense of the past?

PT: Well, that's my idea about it [he laughs]. Or at least that's what I was trying to hint at when I wrote the story. I didn't want to make it all so cut and dried, but I wanted there to be some mystery. How much does he know? How much does he want to know?

CM: Is there the same kind of tension at work in "The Witch of Owl Mountain Springs"?

PT: How so?

CM: Well, the narrator there has a "blank" space—several of them, in fact. There is a whole series of events he can't remember.

PT: Well, yes, in that case then there are some similarities. Again, I've tried to look at how much of the world is concealed from us, and how much we conceal from ourselves.

CM: So the narrator of "The Witch" may not only be concealing from us the terrible truth of the story, but he may also be concealing it from himself?

PT: I think that it's certainly a possibility.

CM: A possibility?

PT: Yes [he laughs]. A possibility.

CM: So two stories, and two characters who deceive themselves about the truth?

PT: Yes, except in "The Witch" there's the added question of whether or not the narrator is trying to deceive us. He may or may not have these moments of amnesia, whereas in "The Oracle," the narrator definitely doesn't remember the War.

CM: So in "The Witch" there's a kind of a double tension at work. The narrator may be deceiving us—intentionally—or he may—unintentionally—be deceiving himself.

PT: Yes.

CM: And there's no way of knowing for sure?

PT: [He smiles.] No. Or at least that's the way I see it.

CM: So I'll have to settle for mystery?

PT: Yes. I want that uncertainty. You see, things can be true on two levels. That's what I always seem to discover as I write my stories. For instance, I'm now writing a story about my two sisters and the two men they married. Growing up, I would listen to stories about them, and the stories they would tell about each other. All four of them were quite important to me. And so I'm starting with the stories I know, the stories I heard. But as I think about them, as I write down the stories, I'm not restricted to only that kind of truth. There's a second kind of truth, the one that I arrive at after thinking through the events. And it's this second level of truth where things get interesting, where you start to really think about things and, finally, why you are thinking about them in that way.

CM: So there's a "historical" truth and then another truth you arrive at after you've worked your imagination upon that truth. At that second "truth"—if I'm understanding you correctly—that second truth can be the mystery of things. It doesn't have to be, but it can be.

PT: Yes. You're not departing from one truth in favor of another. You're not saying what you remember didn't happen. Instead, you're allowing the imagination to take over. This way you don't get caught in the literal events of the story you're trying to understand. At some point the imagination takes over, and you have to let it take over. Earlier, we talked about concealment. Well, sometimes, when the imagination takes over you discover all sorts of interesting things you thought you had forgotten. And that's when you begin to wonder whether you've forgotten them or concealed them [he laughs]. And then you have to decide whether, in writing the story, you are going to write about those things you've forgotten or whether you are going to conceal them. It's all so very interesting, you know: what happened, why did it happen that way, why are you remembering it in a certain way, what have you forgotten, why have you forgotten it? Such great questions.

CM: So, in a way, writing can be seen as pulling secrets out of yourself.

PT: Well, not all writing, but it certainly happens if you let it. Finally, that's what the drama of any story is—finding out what you think about things. Perhaps what you find out is a secret you've been keeping, perhaps not. But you have to let your imagination take over. It's the only way to discover things.

CM: But that leads me to another question. The ending of "The Oracle" reminds me of the ending of *A Summons to Memphis*. Not only is there a reference to Phillip Carver at the end of "The Oracle" . . .

PT: Oh, that's just something I did for fun.

CM: Just for fun, or are we going to see more of Phillip in upcoming stories?

PT: I don't think so. I kind of took the lead from Trollope. Sometimes he would refer to other characters from other books. As a reader, you get a kick out of it, or at least I do.

CM: Well, at the end of "The Oracle," Lila has gone back to D.C. and she is no longer under the spell—that is, if she ever was—and the narrator has married Ruthie Ann and the two of them have moved in with Ruthie Ann's mother. After all of this, in the final paragraph of the story, the narrator says, "We three have lived there very happily together during all the years since, enjoying the uneventful seclusion we are all equally fond of, gardening, reading our favorite fiction, taking turns with the shopping. We have achieved such peace that thoughts about whatever became of Phillip Carver, that other friend who wanted to enlist as a conscientious objector—even such thoughts as that never disturb us here" (88). The sentiments expressed here seem to be just like the sentiments expressed by Phillip at the end of *A Summons to Memphis* when he too withdraws from the world in order to achieve peace. I think Phillip describes himself as "serenely free"?

PT: I think both men have found themselves a tiny little niche in life so that they can carry on. I've always said that defining things allows us to place limits on them, and perhaps limiting things helps us to define them as well. Yes, both men are withdrawing from the world and limiting their lives in the process—and this certainly helps them achieve a sense of peace, of definition, but we must question the kind of peace they've settled for. But as far as actually trying to create stories with a similar ending, as in the case you've raised with *A Summons to Memphis* and "The Oracle at Stoneleigh Court," I don't want to pretend that I'm doing this. Yes, when you raise the issue, I do see some similarities, but you know, sometimes people read stories and begin to interpret them in ways that surprise me. I hadn't really thought about trying to make connections between the two stories. As I said before, I brought in Phillip Carver just for fun.

There was once a teacher down in Florida, Jacksonville, I believe, who had his class write interpretations of "A Walled Garden." He mailed them to me, and some of them I thought were quite brilliant. Oh, the interpretations were all very Freudian. But, the truth was, I didn't know any Freud, and all the while these students were giving me credit for working out and working through Freudian ideas. Now, I suppose I could have taken credit for doing so [he laughs], but why? All these different interpretations made the story very interesting, and interesting in ways I hadn't seen or intended. So when you make a connection between Phillip Carver and the narrator of "The Oracle," it makes the ending of the story interesting, perhaps more interesting than I had intended [he laughs].

CM: You wouldn't be accusing an academic of reading into your work, now would you?

PT: Well, it's all very interesting that we've starting talking about this subject because, as you know, the novel I've just completed involves some of these very issues.

CM: This novel is an extension of the story "Cousin Aubrey," isn't it?

PT: Yes. And the narrator of that novel had wanted, in his youth, to be an artist. But, instead, he became an art critic, an academic. He allows himself to become more interested in the art of others than with his own art, one reason being that it is easier for him to write about what others have created than to create his own art. So, he's taken the easy way out by becoming a critic. The narrator's son, on the other hand, is a true artist. At the end of the novel, the son must break away and strike out on his own.

CM: And this breaking away, it is essential then?

PT: Yes. The heroes who haunt this novel are the people who disappear, like those who went West, or those who were able to become independent, like Cousin Aubrey—whereas the narrator settles for a life of security in the academic village, the son realizes there is more, just as Cousin Aubrey did years ago. The narrator sees the example of Cousin Aubrey and is fascinated by what he has been able to do—to break away from the conventions and expectations he was born into. But the narrator can't; he doesn't have the courage to do this himself, not really do it.

CM: The narrator's fascination with Cousin Aubrey—and here I go again making connections to other stories you've written—but the fascination the narrator shows with Cousin Aubrey reminds me of similar situations in other stories where you have characters fascinated by men and women who are able to just up and disappear. I'm thinking, of course, of an early story like "Miss Leonora When Last Seen" or a more recent one like "The Witch of Owl Mountain Springs."

PT: Well I've always been fascinated by such characters. There are a lot of them in my family history.

CM: Do these characters fascinate you more because they seem to have escaped from something or because they have moved toward something?

PT: It works both ways. At first, they seem to be running away. But then one begins to wonder. Perhaps these people have something special about them, have an imagination that those who stay don't have. If they are seeking something and they are out there somewhere, have they found it? Again, these are ideas I tried to think about in the novel I just finished. Why does Cousin Aubrey leave? Is he running from something or looking for something? What has he found? And the narrator, is it too late for him? And why is he looking for Cousin Aubrey? Is it in order to find out what Cousin Aubrey has learned, or is it because he wants to bring him back into the fold?

CM: In the past, you've described your fiction as being an ongoing discussion with yourself. Sounds like this new novel is much the same.

PT: Exactly. I've said this before, but writing stories allows you to discover what you think about things. I try to come up with some answers when I write, but the discussion, the questions, always seem so much more interesting than the solutions, if I ever get any.

CM: I remember that when I read an early draft of your new novel last summer, you were seeking to answer one big question—what would be the title of the novel? Do you have any answers, or just more questions?

PT: [He laughs.] Only more questions, of course. As you know, when I originally conceived of the novel it was entitled *To the Lost State*. But as I worked on the novel, the focus shifted more to the search for Cousin Aubrey and away from the train ride to the lost state. So I decided to rename the novel *Cousin Aubrey Redux*. Here again, I was taking the lead from Trollope, trying to recall his novel *Phineas Redux*. But, all of sudden, *Cousin Aubrey Redux* became an unsatisfactory title. While I'm not going to go back to *To the Lost State,* I'm searching for a title that suggests some sense of place.

CM: What was it that Hemingway said, if you need a title for a novel, first go to the Bible and then to Shakespeare. Or perhaps it was vice versa?

PT: That's clever advice, but I don't think it's going to help me much unless there's something in Shakespeare about Tennessee [he laughs]. It seems that every time I come up with a good title, there's a reason it's not a good title. For instance, I've been considering a new title lately, *Fugitives*.

CM: *Fugitives?* Academics are going to have a good time with that one.

PT: I know [he laughs]. But of course the moment I think of *Fugitives* as a title, *The Fugitive* comes out as a movie. People keep getting the jump on me. I'll have to see what my editors say. I've played around with a lot of titles, and *Fugitives* helps to highlight many of the concerns I'm working with—imagination, escape, disappearance, art, and art criticism.

CM: And it also suggests a sense of place, a very Tennessee sense of place.

PT: Yes, but we'll see. I'm sure that next week I'll be playing with a new title. Perhaps I'll read more Trollope.

CM: I can see from your desk over there that you're working on other things as well. Would you care to talk about them?

PT: I always have a few stories going, but my new big project—and it seems I always have to have one—my new big project is trying to turn *A Stand in the Mountains* into a novel. And here I'm taking the lead from Red Warren. Most of the time, you write a novel first, and then it becomes a play. I remember that Warren wrote a play called *Proud Flesh,* and it had a chorus of doctors in it. And later, from that material, he wrote *All the King's Men.* I don't know anybody else who has written first a play and then a novel based upon it. As I said, you usually get it the other way.

CM: What has led you back to *A Stand in the Mountains* after all these years?

PT: I've always thought it was a good play, that it deserved an audience. Perhaps changing it into a novel will give it that audience. Who knows, maybe changing it from a play to a novel will encourage someone to produce the play. That would be interesting.

CM: In changing *A Stand in the Mountains* from a play to a novel, are you making any major changes?

PT: Yes, I have to. First, I'm working with a different kind of structure. The play, of course, didn't have a narrator. In the novel-in-progress I've shifted to first-person narration. I'm telling the story from the perspective of the wandering son, the would-be-poet who traveled to Italy in search of his art, but who failed to find it and has returned to the conventional life of Tennessee. Of course, I've had to think more deeply about this character, since I'm filtering this whole world through his perspective. The truth is, at this point at least, I'm struggling with this character a good deal. I'm not sure the kind of mind he has, the kind of intelligence or imagination he possesses. For a while I even played with the idea of making him like Randall Jarrell, to give him the kind of attitude that Jarrell had about conventional people and society. It was fun to see how close I could make him like Jarrell, but in the end, Jarrell was just too intelligent, too perceptive. I'm not sure I want my narrator to be this way at all.

I've changed some of the other characters too. And I've even changed the title from *A Stand in the Mountains* to *Call Me Telemachus*. The new title is straight from the old play. At one point the son says, "Call me Telemachus." The new title helps to focus more on the wandering, the restlessness, of the narrator.

One final thing I'm doing, I'm reworking the introduction to the play. If you remember, I wrote a brief preface to the play in which I explained the history of the mountain and its people. I don't exactly know how this all will work out, but I've taken the preface and split it up into brief sections, about a page each. I've placed these sections at the first of each chapter. It's now understood that these brief sketches are written by Uncle William, the historian. I'm still in the early stages of my revision, and so I'm not sure whether this device will be effective or not, but I think it adds something to the novel. It not only adds background information, but it gives a different tempo to the novel. It may not work. We'll see.

CM: I remember the play being extremely violent, but that all of the violence occurs offstage. Have you thought about the way you are going to handle this violence in your revision?

PT: As it is now, the older brother Harry still shoots his wife, but he does so at the beginning of the novel, whereas in the play this occurs at the very end. It's the violence of his brother that brings the poet back from Italy. It's a different kind of suspense, then. I'm interested in how the narrator handles the violence, how it makes him think about this very conventional world and the disruption it is undergoing.

CM: Perhaps your revision of play into novel will be as successful as Warren's revision of *Proud Flesh* into *All the King's Men*.

PT: Oh, goodness, that would be nice, but I don't think so. Red was always so wonderful with words, in a way that I never really was. Long ago, we would get into discussions, a big group of us, and I'd be stumbling over myself trying to make my point, and then Red would say something and it would be perfect. Of course, he was a very articulate man, more so than I, and he was always so very convincing. He was smart, and he knew how to use words. He loved words and knew how to use them better than anyone I ever knew. I always thought it was a such scandal that he didn't win the Nobel Prize. His breadth, his depth, his everything. He was a superb novelist, a wonderful poet and critic, a playwright. A true rarity. But then again, these prizes don't really mean a thing in the long run. We'd all still be reading *All the King's Men* whether it won the Pulitzer Prize or not. I mean, you can never remember who won last year's awards anyway. For that matter, I don't even remember who wins the Nobel Prize from year to year. I can't even remember the American writers who won it. Faulkner, Hemingway, and a few others, right? [He laughs.] This reminds me, somebody from Memphis I saw recently said to me, "I understand you won the Pulitzer Prize. Did you have to go to Sweden to get it?" And I said, "No, but if someone from Sweden wants to give me a prize, I'll go." [He laughs.] I'm not waiting for a call, however.

CM: In the meantime, you'll just keep on writing?

PT: Certainly. There are still so many stories to think about.

CM: And do you think someday you'll finally ever understand them all?

PT: Oh, maybe one or two perhaps, but all? I hope not.

Works Cited

Booth, Wayne. *The Company We Keep: An Ethics of Fiction.* Berkeley: U of California P, 1988.

Brickhouse, Robert. "Peter Taylor: Writing, Teaching, Making Discoveries." McAlexander, *Conversations* 48–53.

Broadway, J. William. "A Conversation with Peter Taylor." McAlexander, *Conversations* 67–114.

Brown, Ashley. "The Early Fiction of Peter Taylor." *Sewanee Review* 70 (1962): 588–602.

——. "Peter Taylor at Sixty." *Shenandoah* 28 (Winter 1977): 43–53.

Buell, Lawrence. "American Pastoral Ideology Reappraised." *American Literary History* I (1989): 1–29.

Casey, Jane Barnes. "A View of Peter Taylor's Stories." *Virginia Quarterly Review* 54 (Spring 1978): 213–30.

Casey, John. "Peter Taylor as Merlin and Mr. O'Malley." *Shenandoah* 28.2 (Winter 1977): 71–79.

Cather, Willa. *My Antonia.* Boston: Houghton, 1988.

Coffey, Shelby, III. "Sophisticated Fugitive: Peter Taylor and *The New Yorker.*" *Potomac (Washington Post)* 24 Nov. 1968: 23+.

Culler, A. Dwight. "Monodrama and the Dramatic Monologue." *PMLA* 90 (1975): 366–85.

Daniel, Robert. "The Inspired Voice of Mythical Tennessee." McAlexander, *Conversations* 41–47.

Davis, Louise. "Just Who Was That Ward-Belmont Girl Nude in the Closet?" McAlexander, *Conversations* 22–27.

Dean, Ruth. "Peter Taylor: A Private World of Southern Writing." McAlexander, *Conversations* 28–34.

DuPree, Don Keck. "An Interview with Peter Taylor." McAlexander, *Conversations* 54–59.

Ettin, Andrew V. *Literature and the Pastoral.* New Haven: Yale UP, 1984.

Faulkner, William. "Was." In *Go Down, Moses.* New York: Random, 1942.

Ford, Richard. *Wildlife.* New York: Atlantic, 1990.

Freud, Sigmund. *The Psychopathology of Everyday Life.* In *The Standard Edition of the Complete Psychological Works of Sigmund Freud.* Trans. and ed. James Strachey. 24 vols. London: Hogarth, 1953–74. Vol. 6. 1960.

Gareffa, Peter M., and Jean Ross. "Taylor, Peter (Hillsman) 1917–." *Contemporary Authors,* 487–91. New Revision Series 9. Detroit: Gale, 1983.

Goodwin, Stephen. "An Interview with Peter Taylor." McAlexander, *Conversations* 6–21.

———. "Like Nothing Else in Tennessee." *Shenandoah* 28.2 (Winter 1977): 53–58.

Griffith, Albert J. *Peter Taylor.* New York: Twayne Publishers, 1970.

———. *Peter Taylor.* Rev. ed. Boston: Twayne, 1990.

———. "Presences, Absences, and Peter Taylor's Plays." *Shenandoah* 28 (Winter 1977): 62–71.

Grumbach, Doris. "Short Stories to Long Remember." Rev. of *In the Miro District and Other Stories,* by Peter Taylor. *Los Angeles Times* 24 Apr. 1977: 14.

Hamilton, Ian. *Robert Lowell: A Biography.* New York: Random, 1982.

Hulbert, Ann. "Back to the Future." Rev. of *A Summons to Memphis.* McAlexander, *Critical Essays* 66–70.

I'll Take My Stand: The South and the Agrarian Tradition. By Twelve Southerners. New York: Harper, 1930.

Janssen, Marian. *The Kenyon Review 1939–1970, A Critical History.* Baton Rouge: Louisiana State UP, 1990.

Jones, Ernest. *Sigmund Freud: Life and Work.* London: Hogarth, 1953.

Jones, Malcolm. "Mr. Peter Taylor When Last Seen." *Greensboro [N.C.] Daily News/ Record* 27 July 1980: C5.

Kernan, Michael. "Peter Taylor and the Layers of Life." *Washington Post* 4 Mar. 1985: B1+.

Kuehl, Linda Kandel. "Voices and Victims: A Study of Peter Taylor's *In The Miro District.*" Diss. Lehigh U, 1988.

Lacan, Jacques. *Ecrits.* New York: Norton, 1977.

———. "Introduction to the Names-of-the-Father Seminar." *Television: A Challenge to the Psychoanalytic Establishment.* New York: Norton, 1990.

Love, Glen. " 'Et in Arcadia Ego': Pastoral Theory Meets Ecocriticism." *Western American Literature* 27 (Fall 1992): 195–207.

Lytle, Andrew. "On a Birthday." *Shenandoah* 28.2 (1977): 11–17.

MacKethan, Lucinda Hardwick. *The Dream of Arcady: Place and Time in Southern Literature.* Baton Rouge: Louisiana State UP, 1980.

Marx, Leo. *The Machine in the Garden: Technology and the Pastoral Ideal in America.* New York: Oxford UP, 1964.

———. "Pastoralism in America." *Ideology and Classic American Literature.* Ed. Sacvan Bercovitch and Myra Jehlen, 35–69. Cambridge: Cambridge UP, 1986.

McAlexander, Hubert H., ed. *Conversations with Peter Taylor.* Literary Conversations Series. Jackson: UP of Mississippi, 1987.

———, ed. *Critical Essays on Peter Taylor.* New York: Hall, 1993.

Middleman, Louis I. *In Short.* New York: St. Martin's, 1981.

Oates, Joyce Carol. "Realism of Distance, Realism of Immediacy." *Southern Review* 7 (1971): 295–313.

Peden, William. "A Hard and Admirable Toughness: The Stories of Peter Taylor." Robison 153–54.

Pinkerton, Jan. "The Non-Regionalism of Peter Taylor: An Essay Review." *Georgia Review* 24 (1970): 432–40.

Poggioli, Renato. *The Oaten Flute.* Cambridge: Harvard UP, 1975.

Porter, Katherine Anne. *The Collected Essays and Occasional Writings of Katherine Anne Porter.* Boston: Houghton, 1970.

Richards, Robert. "Part of Memphis May Come Alive in Next Novel by Peter Taylor." McAlexander, *Conversations* x.

Robinson, David M. "Summons from the Past." Rev. of *A Summons to Memphis*. McAlexander, *Critical Essays* 55–60.

Robison, James Curry. *Peter Taylor: A Study of the Short Fiction*. Twayne's Studies in Short Fiction. Boston: Twayne, 1988.

Ross, Jean W. Interview. Gareffa and Ross 489–91.

"Short Stories: Their Past, Present and Future." *Publishers' Weekly* 14 Dec. 1970: 12–15.

Sides, W. Hampton. "Interview: Peter Taylor." McAlexander, *Conversations* 129–36.

Smith, Wendy. "*PW* Interviews: Peter Taylor." McAlexander, *Conversations* 60–65.

Stallman, R. W., and Lillian Gilkes, eds. *Stephen Crane: Letters*. New York: NYUP, 1960.

Sullivan, Walter. "The Last Agrarian: Peter Taylor Early and Late." *Sewanee Review* 95 (Spring 1987): 308–17.

Taylor, Peter. *The Collected Stories of Peter Taylor*. New York: Farrar, 1969.

——. *The Early Guest. Shenandoah* 24.2 (Winter 1973): 21–43.

——. *Happy Families Are All Alike*. New York: McDowell, 1959.

——. "The Inspired Voice of Mythical Tennessee: An Interview with Peter Taylor." With Robert Daniel. *Kenyon College Alumni Bulletin* 7 (1983): 18–20.

——. *In the Miro District and Other Stories*. New York: Knopf, 1977.

——. "Knowing." *Agenda* 13.4 and 14.1 (combined issue, Winter/Spring 1976): 97–100.

——. *Literature, Sewanee, and the World: Founders' Day Address 1972*. Sewanee, TN: U of the South, 1972.

——. *A Long Fourth and Other Stories*. New York: Harcourt, 1947.

——. *Miss Leonora When Last Seen and 15 Other Stories*. New York: Obolensky, 1963.

——. *The Old Forest and Other Stories*. Garden City, NY: Dial, 1985.

——. *The Oracle at Stoneleigh Court: Stories*. New York: Knopf, 1993.

——. Personal interview, Sewanee, Tennessee, Hubert H. McAlexander. 10 Aug. 1993.

——. *Presences: Seven Dramatic Pieces*. Boston: Houghton, 1973.

——. "Reminiscences." *The Fugitives, the Agrarians, and Other Twentieth Century Southern Writers*, 17–21. Charlottesville: Alderman Library, U of Virginia P, 1985.

——. *A Stand in the Mountains*. New York: Beil, 1985.

——. *A Summons to Memphis*. New York: Knopf, 1986.

——. *The Widows of Thornton*. New York: Harcourt, 1954.

——. *A Woman of Means*. New York: Harcourt, 1950.

Thompson, Barbara. "Interview with Peter Taylor for *The Paris Review*." McAlexander, *Conversations* 137–73.

Todorov, Tsvetan. *The Poetics of Prose*. Ithaca: Cornell UP, 1977.

Weales, Gerald, ed. *Arthur Miller, "Death of a Salesman": Text and Criticism*. New York: Viking, 1967.

Wilson, Robert. Introduction. *In the Miro District*, 2–4. 2nd Carroll and Graf ed. New York: Carroll, 1987.

Withycombe, E. G. *The Oxford Dictionary of English Christian Names*. 2nd ed. London: Oxford UP, 1950.

Contributors

ANN BEATTIE has published highly acclaimed fiction for nearly two decades. Her work includes *What Was Mine* (stories, 1991), *Picturing Will* (novel, 1989), *Love Always* (novel, 1985), *Secrets & Surprises* (stories, 1978), and *Chilly Scenes of Winter* (novel, 1976).

MADISON SMARTT BELL is writer-in-residence at Goucher College and an adjunct faculty member in the Writing Seminars at The Johns Hopkins University. He is the author of two collections of short stories and seven novels, the most recent of which, *Save Me, Joe Louis,* was published in 1993.

ROBERT H. BRINKMEYER, JR., is a professor of American literature and Southern studies at the University of Mississippi. He has published widely on Southern writers; his books include *Three Catholic Writers of the Modern South, The Art and Vision of Flannery O'Connor,* and, most recently, *Katherine Anne Porter's Artistic Development: Primitivism, Traditionalism, and Totalitarianism.*

CLEANTH BROOKS has been one of the nation's most influential teachers of literary values. Editor, anthologist, university professor, critic, rhetorician, and cultural ambassador, Mr. Brooks is the author of numerous books on poetry, fiction, and drama, among them *Modern Poetry and the Tradition* (1939), *The Well-Wrought Urn* (1947), and four books on William Faulkner. With Robert Penn Warren, he edited the widely used anthologies *Understanding Poetry* (1939) and *Understanding Fiction* (1943).

ALBERT J. GRIFFITH is a professor of English and communication arts at Our Lady of the Lake University. The author of the Twayne Series volume on Peter Taylor, he has also written extensively on American literature, language, education, and culture.

ELIZABETH HARDWICK, distinguished New York novelist, essayist, and editor, is a longtime friend of Peter Taylor. Ms. Hardwick is the author of the novels

The Ghostly Lover, The Simple Truth, and *Sleepless Nights* and essays collected as *A View of My Own: Essays on Literature and Society; Bartleby in Manhattan;* and *Seduction and Betrayal: Women and Literature.* She also edited *The Selected Letters of Henry James.* A member of the American Academy and Institute of Arts and Letters, Hardwick is also a founding editor of *The New York Review of Books.*

LINDA KANDEL KUEHL is an associate professor of English at Delaware Valley College, where she specializes in American literature and modern drama. Her work on Peter Taylor and other contemporary Southern writers has appeared in *Contemporary Literature, Studies in Short Fiction, The Southern Quarterly, The South Carolina Review,* and the *Alabama Literary Review.*

CREIGHTON LINDSAY is a professor of English at Mt. Angel Seminary in Benedict, Oregon. His essay, "Phillip Carver's Ethical Appeal in Peter Taylor's *A Summons to Memphis,*" appeared in the Spring 1991 issue of *The Mississippi Quarterly.*

DAVID H. LYNN, a former student of Peter Taylor's, is a consulting editor of *The Kenyon Review* and an assistant professor of English at Kenyon College. He published *The Hero's Tale: Narrators in the Early Modern Novel* in 1989.

HUBERT H. McALEXANDER holds a Beaver Teaching Professorship at the University of Georgia; he has published numerous articles and reviews and three books: *The Prodigal Daughter* (1981), a biography of the nineteenth-century Mississippi regionalist and feminist Sherwood Bonner; *Conversations with Peter Taylor* (1987); and *Critical Essays on Peter Taylor* (1993).

CHRISTOPHER P. METRESS wrote his Vanderbilt University doctoral dissertation on Peter Taylor. An assistant professor of English at Samford University, he is currently editing *The Critical Response to Dashiell Hammett,* a collection of essays to be published by Greenwood Press.

RONALD J. NELSON is coordinator of technical writing at James Madison University.

LINDA RICHMOND is an assistant professor of English at Essex Community College; she has published articles on Nadine Gordimer, Doris Lessing, and Alice Munro.

DAVID M. ROBINSON is Oregon Professor of English at Oregon State University in Corvallis. His study of Emerson's later work, *Emerson and the Conduct of*

Life, was published in 1993 by Cambridge University Press. He has published essays on Peter Taylor in the *Southern Review* and the *Southern Literary Journal* and is at work on a critical study of Peter Taylor for the University of Georgia Press.

LYNDA B. SALAMON is an associate professor of English and director of the writing center at Essex Community College; she helped organize and was a presenter at the 1991 Peter Taylor Symposium in Baltimore.

WARD SCOTT studied fiction writing with Smith Kirkpatrick at the University of Florida. He lives in Gainesville, where he is an instructor at Santa Fe Community College.

C. RALPH STEPHENS is a professor of English and head of the department of English at Essex Community College. He directed the Peter Taylor Symposium held in Baltimore in April 1991 and edited *The Correspondence of Flannery O'Connor* (1985) and *The Fiction of Anne Tyler* (1990).

ROBERT WILSON, book review editor and columnist for *USA Today,* wrote the introduction for the Carroll and Graf edition of Peter Taylor's *In the Miro District and Other Stories.*

Index